STUDIES IN ECONOMIC AND SOCIAL HISTORY

This series, specially commissioned by the Economic History Society, provides a guide to the current interpretations of the key themes of economic and social history in which advances have recently been made or in which there has been significant debate.

Originally entitled 'Studies in Economic History', in 1974 the series had its scope extended to include topics in social history, and the new series title, 'Studies in Economic and Social History', signalises this development.

The series gives readers access to the best work done, helps them to draw their own conclusions in major fields of study, and by means of the critical bibliography in each book guides them in the selection of further reading. The aim is to provide a springboard to further work rather than a set of pre-packaged conclusions or short-cuts.

ECONOMIC HISTORY SOCIETY

The Economic History Society, which numbers over 3000 members, publishes the *Economic History Review* four times a year (free to members) and holds an annual conference. Enquiries about membership should be addressed to the Assistant Secretary, Economic History Society, Peterhouse, Cambridge. Full-time students may join at special rates.

STUDIES IN ECONOMIC AND SOCIAL HISTORY

Edited for the Economic History Society by T. C. Smout

PUBLISHED

Bill Albert Latin America and the World Economy from Independence to 1930
B. W. E. Alford Depression and Recovery? British Economic Growth, 1918–1939
Michael Anderson Approaches to the History of the Western Family, 1500–1914
P. J. Cain Economic Foundations of British Overseas Expansion, 1815–1914
S. D. Chapman The Cotton Industry in the Industrial Revolution
Neil Charlesworth British Rule and the Indian Economy, 1800–1914
J. A. Chartres Internal Trade in England, 1500–1700
R. A. Church The Great Victorian Boom, 1850–1873
D. C. Coleman Industry in Tudor and Stuart England
P. L. Cottrell British Overseas Investment in the Nineteenth Century
Ralph Davis English Overseas Trade, 1500–1700
M. E. Falkus The Industrialisation of Russia, 1700–1914
Peter Fearon The Origins and Nature of the Great Slump, 1929–1932
T. R. Gourvish Railways and the British Economy, 1830–1914
Robert Gray The Aristocracy of Labour in Nineteenth-century Britain, 1850–1900
John Hatcher Plague, Population and the English Economy, 1348–1530
J. R. Hay The Origins of the Liberal Welfare Reforms, 1906–1914
R. H. Hilton The Decline of Serfdom in Medieval England
E. L. Jones The Development of English Agriculture, 1815–1873
John Lovell British Trade Unions, 1875–1933
J. D. Marshall The Old Poor Law, 1795–1834
Alan S. Milward The Economic Effects of the Two World Wars on Britain
G. E. Mingay Enclosure and the Small Farmer in the Age of the Industrial Revolution
Rosalind Mitchison British Population Change Since 1860
R. J. Morris Class and Class Consciousness in the Industrial Revolution, 1780–1850
A. E. Musson British Trade Unions, 1800–1875
R. B. Outhwaite Inflation in Tudor and Early Stuart England
R. J. Overy The Nazi Economic Recovery, 1932–1938
P. L. Payne British Entrepreneurship in the Nineteenth Century
G. D. Ramsay The English Woollen Industry, 1500–1750
Michael E. Rose The Relief of Poverty, 1834–1914
Michael Sanderson Education, Economic Change and Society in England 1780–1870
S. B. Saul The Myth of the Great Depression, 1873–1896
Arthur J. Taylor Laissez-faire and State Intervention in Nineteenth-century Britain
Peter Temin Causal Factors in American Economic Growth in the Nineteenth Century
Margaret Walsh The American Frontier Revisited

OTHER TITLES ARE IN PREPARATION

Enclosures in Britain 1750–1830

Prepared for
The Economic History Society by

MICHAEL TURNER
Lecturer in Economic History
University of Hull

MACMILLAN PRESS
LONDON

First published 1984 by
THE MACMILLAN PRESS LTD
London and Basingstoke
Companies and representatives
throughout the world

Typeset by
Wessex Typesetters Ltd
Frome, Somerset

Printed in Hong Kong

British Library Cataloguing in Publication Data
Turner, M. E.
Enclosure in Britain, 1750–1830.—
(Studies in economic and social history)
1. Inclosures
I. Title   II. Series
33.7′6   HD594.6

ISBN 0–333–31682–7

Contents

Author's Acknowledgements and Note on References   7

Editor's Preface   8

List of Tables   9

List of Figures   9

1 Introduction
    (i) Definition   11
    (ii) Historiographical Note   12

2 Enclosure in Time and Space
    (i) England   16
    (ii) A Note on Wales   26
    (iii) Scotland   28
    (iv) A Note on Non-Parliamentary Enclosure   33

3 Enclosure and Investment: The Decision to Enclose
    (i) General Factors   36
    (ii) The Open Fields: Inflexible or Adaptable?   37
    (iii) Productivity Gains and Enclosure   39
    (iv) Rent and Productivity Gains   41
    (v) Cost-Benefit   44
    (vi) Other Economic Considerations   46

4 Investment and Cost: Part 1, The Economic Cost
    (i) The Total Cost   53
    (ii) Distribution of Public Costs   60

5   Investment and Cost: Part 2, The Social Cost
      (i)   Social Consequences: The Background to the
              Debate   64
     (ii)   J. D. Chambers and Revision   67
    (iii)   Revisionism, Counter-Revised   71
     (iv)   The Recent Debates   73
      (v)   Enclosure and Labour Supply   76

6   Conclusions   81

    Bibliography   84

    Index   94

Acknowledgements

MY thanks to Brenda Buchanan, Dr R. C. Allen and Dr J. Chapman for the opportunity to see their work in advance of publication. Jan Crowther and Colin Munro respectively gave me an item of information and a reference which perfectly illustrated important points in the script and for which I am grateful. Professor T. C. Smout and Dr I. D. Whyte gave me valuable advice in constructing the Scottish bibliography, and Professor Smout also gave me instruction about Scottish rural tenurial relationships. Derek Waite drew the maps and diagrams. I am particularly indebted to Professor Smout for his editorial guidance which transformed an excessively long first draft into a script of pamphlet size.

MICHAEL TURNER

Note on References

References in the text within square brackets refer to the numbered items in the bibliography. Colons separate italicised page numbers from their appropriate references and semicolons separate different references.

Editor's Preface

SINCE 1968, when the Economic History Society and Macmillan published the first of the 'Studies in Economic and Social History', the series has established itself as a major teaching tool in universities, colleges and schools, and as a familiar landmark in serious bookshops throughout the country. A great deal of the credit for this must go to the wise leadership of its first editor, Professor M. W. Flinn, who retired at the end of 1977. The books tend to be bigger now than they were originally, and inevitably more expensive; but they have continued to provide information in modest compass at a reasonable price by the standards of modern academic publications.

There is no intention of departing from the principles of the first decade. Each book aims to survey findings and discussion in an important field of economic or social history that has been the subject of recent lively debate. It is meant as an introduction for readers who are not themselves professional researchers but who want to know what the discussion is all about – students, teachers and others generally interested in the subject. The authors, rather than either taking a strongly partisan line or suppressing their own critical faculties, set out the arguments and the problems as fairly as they can, and attempt a critical summary and explanation of them from their own judgement. The discipline now embraces so wide a field in the study of the human past that it would be inappropriate for each book to follow an identical plan, but all volumes will normally contain an extensive descriptive bibliography.

The series is not meant to provide all the answers but to help readers to see the problems clearly enough to form their own conclusions. We shall never agree in history, but the discipline will be well served if we know what we are disagreeing about, and why.

T. C. SMOUT

University of St Andrews   *Editor*

List of Tables

I The Supply of Parliamentary Enclosure 1730–1844   20
II Chronology and Summary of English Parliamentary
    Enclosure   21
III Public Cost of Parliamentary Enclosure in England
    1730–1844   57
IV Distribution of Enclosure Costs in Warwickshire and
    Buckinghamshire   62

List of Figures

1 Chronology of Parliamentary Enclosure in England
    1750–1819   18–19
2 Common and Waste Enclosed as a Percentage of County
    Area c.1750–1870   22
3 The Enclosure of the Open Fields as a Percentage of County
    Area c.1750–1870   25
4 Trends in Wheat Prices and Interest Rates 1731–1819   48–9

1 Introduction

(i) DEFINITION

THE term enclosure mainly refers to that land reform which transformed a traditional method of agriculture under systems of co-operation and communality in communally administered holdings, usually in large fields which were devoid of physical territorial boundaries, into a system of agricultural holding in severalty by separating with physical boundaries one person's land from that of his neighbours. This was, then, the disintegration and reformation of the open fields into individual ownership. Inter alia enclosure registered specific ownership, adjudicated on shared ownership (for example by identifying and separating common rights), and declared void for all time communal obligations, privileges and rights. Enclosure also meant the subdivision of areas of commons, heaths, moors, fens and wastes into separate landholdings and again involved the abandonment of obligations, privileges and rights.

There was enormous regional variability in enclosure. For example, there were different ways of raising a boundary, from the quickset hedges of the Midlands, in vivid contrast to the heavy stone walls of the Pennines, and the combination of enclosure and drainage schemes in the fens of Lincolnshire, Norfolk, Cambridgeshire and Somerset often producing ditches rather than fences. In some highland areas physical boundaries were not constructed at all but instead there was reassessment of stinting rights (for example a reassessment of the number of sheep that could be depastured on a given area of land). In Scotland, as we shall see, enclosure could mean something entirely different again.

This pamphlet is concerned mainly with parliamentary enclosure, that is enclosure conducted by the instrument of an Act of Parliament. Men known as commissioners were employed to divide the communal interests of the parish, township, etc., among the claimants of those interests, and to lay out the courses of new roads, footpaths, bridlepaths and tracks. These men were nominated by the major

11

interests in the parish, by the church in its position as a major owner of the tithes, by the lord of the manor as the owner of the rights of the soil, and by the majority in value of the freeholders. The commissioners employed a battery of administrators, surveyors, clerks, bankers, and so on. The parliamentary proceedings and the subsequent administration of enclosure are well explained elsewhere [98]. The procedures were complicated to the extent that enclosure could be privately and locally sponsored, and publicly and locally applied, or generally applied. Thus private acts, public acts, and general acts resulted. In the cases of the first two methods active application was made to Parliament, but the third was most frequently a case of creating a set of conditions or regulations which encouraged local applications to be made [see 10: *esp. 28–34*].

We must emphasise early on that enclosure, involving as it did the shift from communal ownership and husbandry into individual ownership and husbandry, was far more complicated than this brief introduction suggests. In addition, the open fields and commons and wastes that were enclosed were by no means a static, unchanging method of ownership and husbandry but should be viewed in terms of an evolving system in which enclosure was the final item of change. Chapter 2 will explore the geographical and temporal variations in parliamentary enclosure, and the important exception of enclosure by non-legislative means. Chapter 3 will question the necessity for enclosure, whether it was stimulated by the promise of economic gains in prevailing economic conditions. Chapter 4 will look at the cost of enclosure and Chapter 5 will discuss the social consequences of enclosure.

(ii) HISTORIOGRAPHICAL NOTE

Long-held popular beliefs related to the economic, social and political background and consequences of enclosure have relatively recently been overturned. Historiographically there are three uneven periods: a pre-1914 phase of cataloguing and interpreting, often with a pessimistic note in regard to the social consequences; a phase of revisionism and much local history enthusiasm beginning in the 1930s and continuing well into the post-Second World War era, sounding a more optimistic note; and lastly a phase still in motion, which in many ways is counter-revisionist because it is confronting the broadest issues thrown up by research with greater clarity and more secure data. This note is concerned with the first period while the arguments in later chapters bring the historiography up to date.

To begin at the beginning, or in our case the beginning of the end, the first decade or so of the twentieth century marked both the end of enclosure in Britain, practically speaking, and the beginning of great speculation as to its impact. To some extent enclosure is not yet complete and within the framework of existing law it never will be. The 1965 Commons Registration Act called for the local registration of commons over the period 1967–72 and fossilised the last vestiges of what was once a more extensively 'open' Britain [13 and 14 Eliz.II, c.64, 1965]. From 1972 onwards over one million acres of common in England was recorded and its status safeguarded for the foreseeable future, though there is a move by some landowners to have these commons deregistered and enclosed behind fences [*Sunday Times*, 26 July 1981: 4].

The enclosure of the Gloucestershire parish of Elmstone Hardwicke in 1914 effectively marked the end of British enclosing activity, though more realistically we should consider the enclosure movement complete by about 1870. Our first phase of writing on enclosures therefore came in the wake of the enclosure movement, but sufficiently detached from its principal thrusts a hundred or more years earlier for a relatively unromantic, disinterested view to be obtained. The spatial impact of enclosure was first quantified by Slater in his *The English Peasantry and the Enclosure of Common Fields* (1907). It remained for long the standard reference though we now accept that it underestimated the enclosure of common and waste by a large margin. A more accurate statement was Gonner's *Common Land and Inclosure* (1912). He mapped his evidence at the level of the registration district and rightly those maps have become standard interpretations of the distribution of enclosure. This was a wider history of enclosure than Slater with almost as much emphasis on the origins and operation of British agrarian systems as on their periods of dissolution from medieval times onwards.

Accompanying these two classics of cataloguing and description were a number of other studies which were more concerned with interpretation. Johnson's *The Disappearance of the Small Landowner* (1909) was a particularly inspired piece of interpretation because it approached a particular problem involving a special socio-economic group. It also involved an otherwise forgotten primary source which

13

was contemporary with the dominant period of parliamentary enclosure, the land tax of 1780–1832 [see also 21].

Of these early twentieth-century agricultural histories the greatest impact was left by the Hammonds' *The Village Labourer* (1911). Their message was set in overt political terms as part of a trilogy of work on the process of proletarianisation in Britain. Part of their popularity was born out of a contemporary political awareness of the ambiguity of property rights and the intractable process of inheritance. When it came to the peasant inheritance of something so essential as common rights it was seemingly subject to such cursory consideration by squire, church, and parliament at enclosure as to make a mockery of any concept of equity. This was the tone of the Hammonds' argument, reinforced by persuasive if biased evidence of injustices. This evidence has been re-examined periodically and the Hammonds' views tempered considerably, though the latest researches have partially rehabilitated much of their message.

The Hammonds were not alone in their discourse on property rights. Marx also chose the British experience in outlining a theory of capitalism and contemporaries of the Hammonds also spoke in terms of the inequity of capitalist revolutions, whether agrarian or industrial.

The basic tools of research of early investigators were the digests of statistics found in the parliamentary Blue Books, particularly the 1914 *Return in Chronological Order of all Acts passed for the Inclosure of Commons and Wastes* [9; see also 8]. In spite of its misleading title the Commons refers to common fields. It was the best of the official digests though it contains a number of errors and omissions. The productivity of scholarship during the first decade or so of the twentieth century gave successive scholars a valuable reference library. It is only in relatively recent times that some of the basic facts and information have been found incomplete, unreliable or misleading. Curtler's *The Enclosure and Redistribution of our Land* (1920) was about the only new major work to deal with enclosures nationally until Tate made new acreage estimates for 27 of the 42 English counties between 1935–51 [listed in 2: *27–9*; and 10: *4–5*]. Tate also produced a large number of enclosure-related studies [listed in 10: *4*]. From 1951 until his death in 1968 he tried to complete the county handlists to bring them together in a single volume of revised English statistics. The work was completed posthumously, the summary statistics setting out the broad spatial and temporal features of English parliamentary enclosure as we now understand them [10; 107].

As an aid to the most recent historiography the reader should note the relatively recent appearance of a bibliography on enclosures and the open fields; two review essays, one with an appended bibliography; and a bibliography of theses and dissertations on British agrarian history [2; 1; 4; 3].

2 Enclosure in Time and Space

IT is unclear why parliamentary enclosure became the dominant method of enclosure by the mid-eighteenth century in preference to existing methods. The first act was for the enclosure of Radipole in Dorset in 1604, but acts do not become common until well into Georgian times. Perhaps the success of enclosure by local agreement among interested parties in the century or so up to the eighteenth gave way quite naturally to a firmer instrument. Perhaps the subdivision of rights became more complicated and perhaps there were more interested parties which necessitated the decision of a referee to separate claims of ownership. Perhaps there was opposition to enclosure or squabbling over the spoils, making an instrument of parliament necessary and inevitable. Whatever the reason, parliamentary enclosure dominated after c.1750. But we must emphasise that enclosure *per se* was not new; it had been the method of dividing the open fields for centuries. In some counties mere vestiges of the open fields remained to be enclosed by the mid-eighteenth century and in other areas agriculture had not been pursued in open fields, and so a cross-section across Britain would reveal the whole evolutionary history of agriculture from complete open field arrangements to enclosed farms and fields sometimes of long or ancient origin.

Parliamentary enclosure was important in England and Wales but Scotland must be treated separately with much enclosure in that country enacted under laws which antedated the Union with England in 1707, though in fact most of the enclosure occurred after Union. Additionally we must attempt an estimate (qualitative rather than quantitative) of non-parliamentary enclosure.

In England there were over 5250 private or public acts of enclosure or individual enclosures under the umbrella of the nineteenth-century general acts. The parliamentary enclosure of open fields, commons, wastes, etc., was predominantly by private local acts and can be more narrowly placed between 1750–1850 or even 1750–1830. Over 85 per cent of all parliamentary enclosure was complete or on the statute book by 1830, but to stop in 1830 excludes all of the mid- and late-nineteenth-century enclosure under the authority of the General Acts of 1836, 1840 and 1845. In some areas such enclosure was very important, though only in Cambridgeshire and Oxfordshire did post-1830 parliamentary enclosure amount to more than 10 per cent of county area [107: *186–95*].

Figure 1 captures the chronology of the main thrusts of English parliamentary enclosure. Quite clearly it was not one but two movements, each of which in a number of ways was quite distinctive. They were different in a spatial sense, in a chronological sense, and also in an economic sense because we can identify different motivating forces behind the enclosures. In the spatial sense there were parts of East Anglia where parliamentary enclosure had barely begun by 1790 [see 27: *197*], as was also the case in much of West Sussex [49: *75–7*], but in other parts of the country (Northamptonshire, Warwickshire, and Leicestershire) most parliamentary enclosure was over by this date [107: *72–6*]. Such a chronological dispersion increases the difficulty of debating the social and economic record of parliamentary enclosure.

Of all acts 38 per cent were concentrated in the first wave of activity between c.1755–80. The peak year of activity was 1777 when 92 acts were passed and the busiest half decade was the late 1770s when 321 acts were passed. The second peak of activity occurred between 1790 and the mid-1830s, though more importantly it was concentrated during the period of the French Revolutionary and Napoleonic wars. Nine of the ten busiest years in parliamentary enclosure history occur in this period, and the first half of the 1810s was the busiest half decade of all when 547 acts were passed. The war years accounted for 43 per cent of all parliamentary enclosures. It was also a period when marginal land was increasingly brought into regular or regulated cultivation [56; 139]. With subsequent nineteenth-century incursions into marginal lands the commons and wastes of England and Wales were reduced to trivial proportions [112].

Thus two movements of roughly equal duration and size can be recognised. The first movement embraced mainly, though not exclusively, the heavier soiled counties of the Midland clay belts in Northamptonshire, Warwickshire, Leicestershire and the east and south-east Midlands in general. It also included the lighter clays of

Figure 1

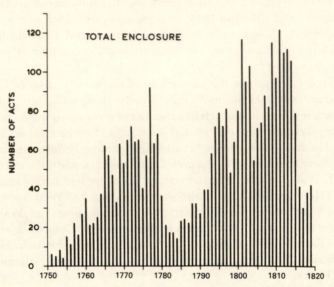

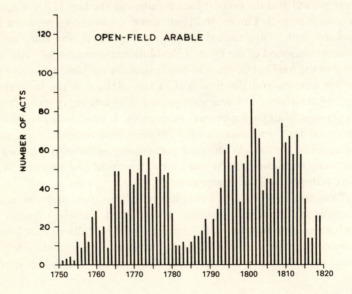

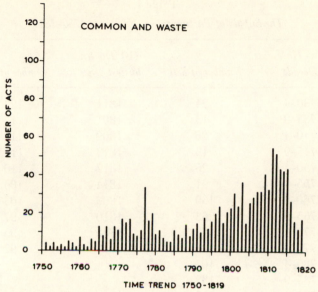

Figure 1 Chronology of Parliamentary Enclosure in England 1750–1819

Source: M. E. Turner, *English Parliamentary Enclosure* (1980), p. 70

much of Lincolnshire and over 60 per cent of East Riding acts. The second movement completed the enclosure of these heavier soils and also included the lighter soils of East Anglia, Lincolnshire, and the East Riding, the marginal soils of the Pennine uplands in West Yorkshire, the Lake District of Cumbria, and the heaths of the southern counties (Surrey, Berkshire, Middlesex).

This division into the arable and the marginal soils, or more correctly into open fields and commons and wastes, can be given greater quantitative expression, as was Tate's intention, but in baldly separating the open fields from the commons and wastes he may have created more problems than he solved because so often the enclosures were composite land reforms involving many land use types (arable, regulated pasture, open pasture, uncultivated commons, genuine wastes and others) [in general see 50; see also 48; 49]. The fact that enclosures were often composite land reforms produces an overestimation of the arable and an underestimation of the common and waste [50]. Another problem is highlighted from a Wiltshire study showing

19

Table I
The Supply of Parliamentary Enclosure 1730–1844

(a) Half Decade	Number of acts	(b) The ten busiest years	Number of acts
1730–4	24	1811	122
1735–9	15	1801	117
1740–4	26	1809	115
1745–9	13	1813	112
1750–4	26	1812	110
1755–9	91	1814	106
1760–4	130	1803	103
1765–9	263	1810	97
1770–4	319	1802	95
1775–9	321	1777	92
1780–4	105		
1785–9	132		
1790–4	235		
1795–9	344		
1800–4	450		
1805–9	430		
1810–14	547		
1815–19	232		
1820–4	115		
1825–9	101		
1830–4	66		
1835–9	59		
1840–4	62		

Source: M. E. Turner, *English Parliamentary Enclosure* (1980), pp. 67–8.

that Tate overstated the arable by including pasture in the arable acreage, either in the form of commons and wastes or as meadow and regulated pasture [152; 7–8]. Following from this is the problem of whether fallows, either temporary or semi-permanent, should be considered as commons and wastes in the sense of unused land, or as pastures however temporary, or as arable because they were potentially arable or involved in what was essentially an arable régime.

Notwithstanding these problems, until the next major revision of statistics is undertaken, Table II is the current summary of enclosure statistics which is available.

Table II
Chronology and Summary of English Parliamentary Enclosure

	Total	Open field arable	Common and waste
Acts	5,265	3,093	2,172
Acres (millions)	6.8	4.5	2.3
Percentage of England	20.9	13.8	7.1
	Acres (millions)	Acres (millions)	Acres (millions)
Pre-1793	2.6	1.9	0.7
1793-1815	2.9	2.0	0.9
1816–1829	0.4	0.2	0.1
Pre-1830	5.8	4.1	1.8
Percentage of England enclosed in the following periods:			
Pre-1793	7.9	5.7	2.2
1793–1815	8.9	6.1	2.8
1816–1829	1.2	0.7	0.4
Pre-1830	18.0	12.6	5.4

Source: M. E. Turner, *English Parliamentary Enclosure* (1980), pp. 62, 71.
Note: The figures are subject to rounding errors.

Williams has focused attention on the eighteenth- and nineteenth-century wastelands of England and Wales and revised upwards the estimation of the amount of land which was reclaimed and brought under regulated cultivation, whether by enclosure, drainage or whatever [112–14]. In 1800 perhaps 21 per cent of England and Wales was wasteland. Locationally it was simply related to physical geography with a heavy concentration in highland Britain where soils

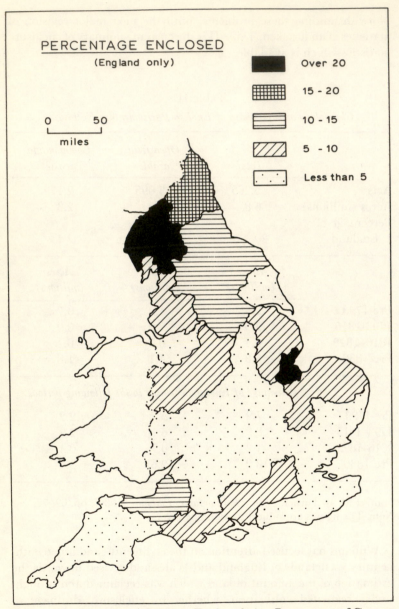

PERCENTAGE ENCLOSED
(England only)

Over 20
15 - 20
10 - 15
5 - 10
Less than 5

0   50
miles

Figure 2   Common and Waste Enclosed as a Percentage of County
Area (England only), c.1750–1870
Source: M. E. Turner, *English Parliamentary Enclosure* (1980), p. 61

were poor and thin, and where there was broken relief and high rainfall. The greatest concentration of waste was in the six northern counties (related to the Lakes and the Pennines), in Wales, and in the south-west of England (the moors). In fact in central Wales in 1800 waste represented 40 per cent and more of land area. Elsewhere the main areas of waste occurred in the fenlands of eastern England and on the heaths and sands of the southern counties [112: *58–9*]. Figure 2 shows the amount of common and waste enclosed as a percentage of county area, c.1750–1870. By the 1870s these wastes had largely been eliminated from the lowlands of eastern and southern England and had been reduced by half in the uplands and in Wales [ibid.: *60*]. By 1873 perhaps only 6–7 per cent of England and Wales was still wasteland.

When was the main attack on the wastes conducted? 'It was the wars with France. . . , that brought about an increased awareness of the value of the waste, and the conquest of the waste and the conquest of France became synonymous in some minds' [ibid.: *57*]. Sir John Sinclair, the President of the Board of Agriculture, said in 1803: 'Let us not be satisfied with the liberation of Egypt, or the subjugation of Malta, but let us subdue Finchley Common; let us conquer Hounslow Heath, let us compel Epping Forest to submit to the yoke of improvement' [quoted in ibid.: *57*]. The wastes were reduced from something like one-fifth to one-fifteenth of the land area of England and Wales in the first three-quarters of the nineteenth century [for examples from Somerset see 113–14; and for Durham see 63]. Enclosure was not the only agent of reclamation, but it was clearly one of the most important.

Enclosure of commons and wastes should not be regarded as a once and for all process which once identified can be catalogued and locked away in a chronological time capsule. The commons and wastes should be seen as a tidal margin which retreated up the hillside, on to the heath and moor, and into the fen, during times of relative land shortage (perhaps in response to population change), or rising prices; to advance again during times of depression or static or falling population. Evidence of the plough quite high up the Peak is indicative of arable cultivation as far back as medieval times on soil and topography that ordinarily was better suited to grazing in rough or permanent pastures. The steep slopes of the uplands remained as rough pasture until between the sixteenth and eighteenth centuries when 'improvements in farm implements and a desire to improve the quality of the stock made the enclosure of some of these steeper commons desirable' [56: *61–74* but esp. *72*]. Similar processes were at play in Scotland, in Wales during the Napoleonic wars, in Somerset and in the reclamation of the Durham Pennines [139; 99: *130–41*; 114: *108–9*; 63: *95–6*]. The reclamation of the Devonian wastes in the two and half centuries before 1800 was evidence of an economic margin related to population change, though more importantly and indirectly to the good fortunes of the local woollen industry [65: *91*]. Much of the advance into and enclosure of the marginal lands was inspired by the inflationary profits of the Napoleonic wars.

Figure 3 maps the density of distribution of open field arable enclosure for the English counties. It is the complement of Figure 2, though for reasons explained earlier it is likely that some common and waste has been mistakenly classified as arable. The map shows the intensive enclosure of open fields within a distorted triangular-shaped area with Gloucestershire at the peak and the East Riding, Lincolnshire and Norfolk at the base, mainly after 1750 and before 1870.

There were considerable county and regional variations. In Suffolk most enclosure was concentrated in the west on the Cambridgeshire border and close to the heartland of the Midlands open fields [107: *46–50*]. In West Sussex enclosure was also limited in extent. The south-western end of the Sussex coastal plain was enclosed in two periods either side of the Napoleonic wars while the eastern end with the neighbouring lowlands and the land to the north of the Downs was enclosed during the war. The Weald and the Downs were enclosed later in the nineteenth century, mainly after 1845 [49: *73–88*, esp. *75*]. In Somerset most enclosure occurred before the eighteenth century and what remained was the great commons and wastes of the low-lying Somerset fenland Levels, the Mendip Hills, and the southern and western hills [113; 114]. Exceptionally, an early enclosure of these commons was in train in the 1770s, before the Napoleonic period. In the western hills there was a second wave of enclosing activity in the period 1830–70 [114: *103*]. Over 40 per cent of Somerset enclosures involved the Levels and were drainage schemes as much as they were enclosures [see also *39*].

In Northumberland and Durham the common arable fields were concentrated in the eastern third of these counties, on the coastal plain at altitudes below 400 feet, with some western penetration along the major valleys of the Tyne and Tees. The Pennines were virtually devoid of common arable fields. Most of the 70–80,000 acres enclosed

24

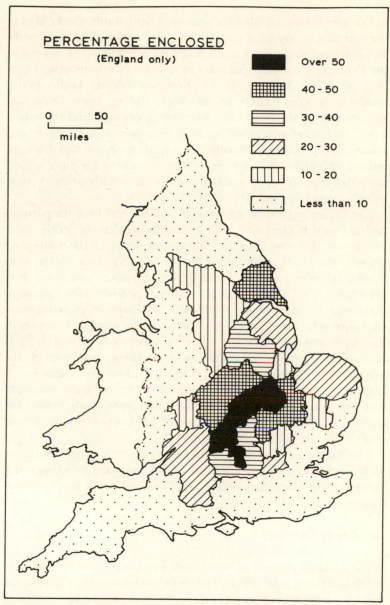

PERCENTAGE ENCLOSED
(England only)

■	Over 50
▦	40 - 50
▤	30 - 40
▨	20 - 30
▥	10 - 20
⋯	Less than 10

0   50
miles

Figure 3   The Enclosure of the Open Fields as a Percentage of
County Area (England only), c.1750–1870
Source: M. E. Turner, *English Parliamentary Enclosure* (1980), p. 59

in Durham between 1550–1750 was open field arable and located in the east, and nearly all of the 107,000 acres enclosed by eighteenth- and nineteenth-century statutes was common and waste located in the Pennines. A similar pattern emerges for Northumberland [63: *84–5, 87–8* for Durham; 40 for Northumberland; 41 for both]. Similarly in Wensleydale in the West Riding, open fields had disappeared by the end of the seventeenth century, and the subsequent enclosures concerned various descriptions of common and waste [57: esp. *172*]. In Lincolnshire, variations in soil and drainage influenced soil fertility, which in turn accounted for quite widely separated chronology of enclosure even for neighbouring or near neighbour parishes [82; 61; 68].

The Felden in south Warwickshire was different from the pastoral Arden Forest in the north, and within the Felden the fertile Avon valley was different from the intractable clays of the south-east towards the Northamptonshire border [77: *19*]. This variation in Warwickshire can also be traced into Staffordshire and Worcestershire [88: *191–4*]. In the champion country of south Worcestershire there were extensive open fields with a density of parliamentary enclosure as high as 43 per cent, whereas in the woodland country in the north and west it was as low as 4 per cent [116: *157–8*]. If Staffordshire can be regarded as a northern extension of the woodlands of Worcestershire and Warwickshire then there was a reasonably uniform enclosure history for the region. Early enclosure had practically denuded the Staffordshire open fields before the eighteenth century so that only about 3 per cent of the county was enclosed by act [88: *204*, *209*; see also 115].

This exercise of dissecting the countryside within the counties or within broad agricultural regions could be repeated for many other areas in many other chronologies, but the point is well made without further detail.

(ii) A NOTE ON WALES

While a similar analysis of Welsh enclosures is possible [for example at the local level as in 100–1] it remains unsatisfactory as long as the basic statistics remain unrevised. At the moment the best available are Bowen's of 1914 with additions made by Jones in 1959 [6; 7]. There were about 250 enclosure acts for the Principality of which only 12 were enacted before the 1790s. There was a Napoleonic wars' peak of activity when 93 acts were passed and a second peak under the powers of the 1845 General Act resulting in extensive enclosure in the 1850s and 1860s when 89 acts were passed [107: *216*]. There is some ambiguity over the amount of land that was enclosed. Some evidence suggests nearly one million acres of mainly common and waste was involved. This sounds high and would have meant the enclosure of 20 per cent of the land area. A second estimate of 385,000 acres is more reasonable [6: *11–13*]. The enclosures of the war period accounted for 200,000 acres or one-eighth of the land then lying in common and waste [99: *32–3*]. We must remember, however, that much of Wales remains commons or wastes as regulated or unregulated pastures.

One of the crucial differences between Welsh and English enclosures was the nature of the terrain and the accompanying land uses. There was a dominance of commons and wastes in Wales. Thomas's point is well taken; in the uplands,

> where pastoral farming had always been predominant, the economy itself was not fundamentally modified, although the detail of its practice was considerably changed . . . what the enclosure movement did for these regions was to abolish the usage of common grazing, and to divide the old commons into blocks of land, which were then allotted according to the claims of those landowners who had previously exercised grazing rights. [100: *27*]

The emphasis was on improving existing animal husbandry rather than changing to arable production, even during the Napoleonic wars when much of pastoral England became arable. To categorise Welsh enclosures as the enclosure of commons and waste therefore is in some ways misleading, they were always an essential part of a pastoral economy supplying the low-lying farms with much needed grazing [101: *27*]. This is a point to bear in mind with respect to other so-called 'wasteland enclosures' elsewhere in Britain, such as the commons above Wensleydale [57: *173*].

In general, during the peak of activity at the time of the Napoleonic wars, the moorland edge was developed irregularly by enclosure and encroachment, though there was not necessarily a great improvement in the economy of the uplands as a result [99: *160*]. There was a similar enclosure of the coastal wastes and the low-lying marshes and valleys. Even when common fields were enclosed it is evident they were often in pasture or used in a system of pastoral husbandry, rather than in arable farming [ibid.: *130–41*].

(iii) Scotland

Late seventeenth-century Scotland was a vastly different place from the Scotland we know today:

> In place of a chequerboard of separate fields one must imagine the ground everywhere lying as open as moorland . . . seldom divided in any way by hedge, wall or dyke . . . The pastoral land . . . was all more or less rough brown waste: there was no question of grass being cultivated as a crop. The ploughed land within was a series of undulating strips or rigs. [141: *120*]

This general scene stands in contrast to England during the same period, with different topography and land use: even the commonality of open field farming, dear to English agrarian history, was present in Scotland but in a fundamentally distinct form. The Scottish enclosure movement, when it came, was a major transformation of the agricultural economy and society and apparently was a very rapid one. It was also very late by English standards. Enclosures of any sort were scarcely known until late in the seventeenth century, though by then much of England had already been enclosed.

A recent lively debate has discussed the 'evolutionary' as distinct from the 'revolutionary' changes in Scotland after the mid-seventeenth century [147; 136; 138; 121; 149]. In the debate enclosure could not be properly separated from other aspects of agrarian reform. Certainly the popularised picture of Scotland in c.1750 as a backward agricultural country is under intense scrutiny, but whether the identification of new crops, new techniques, enclosures, etc., from the mid-seventeenth century onwards is sufficient to establish chronological turning points is open to doubt. It is an issue which has taxed historians of the English agricultural revolution and remains inconclusive on certain issues. In Scotland similar problems occur. Adams, in contrast to Whittington's argument for evolution over a long period, emphasises the narrow chronology of the Scottish agricultural revolution, including enclosure, and in particular the post-Jacobite concentration of the revolution [120: *15*; 121]. Caird establishes that a new rural landscape was deliberately created by revolution rather than evolution, mainly in the eighteenth and nineteenth centuries, in which enclosure was only a part of more expansive agricultural changes [123: *72–3*]. Lebon's study of Ayrshire and Renfrewshire emphasised the rapid revolutionary transformation of the agrarian landscape in the eighteenth century, even though important evolutionary processes were traced well back into the seventeenth century [135: *100–1*]. Gray's wider survey similarly recognised the early origin of individual elements of agrarian reform, but nevertheless focused attention on the drama of change, not simply in the late eighteenth century but in many instances well into the nineteenth century [131; see also 130].

It is not clear from the debate how far the evolutionists wish to overturn the revolutionist school, or whether they simply wish to establish that c.1750 Scottish agriculture was far from backward. In any event, a brief review of enclosure may help to resolve some of the chronology and untangle some of the processes.

There seems little doubt that Scottish enclosures were primarily an eighteenth-century phenomenon by which infield-outfield was replaced by a geometrical field pattern within which the system of runrig was obliterated [119: *252*]. The general enclosure of the lowland estates began in earnest in many areas in the 1760s and 1770s and that of the uplands at the end of the eighteenth century [124: *205*]. It is tempting to draw a parallel with the open field enclosures of the English Midlands after the mid-eighteenth century and the increasing enclosure activity of wastes and commons during the Napoleonic wars, but, as we shall see, what was undergoing enclosure and the meaning of enclosure in Scotland was quite different.

The origin of Scottish enclosure certainly lay before 1750 however, in a late-seventeenth-century process which followed the fashion and interest of the wealthier landowners and was related to the evolution of country houses, hardly touching the tenantry directly. Whyte contrasts the utilitarian English enclosure agreements with the fashion-inspired Scottish counterparts; profit was not completely ignored by Scottish landowners but it has been suggested that conspicuous consumption was more important. This early enclosure in any case was not on a large scale and each project rarely exceeded 250–350 acres, creating 'islands of improvement in a sea of open-field, infield-outfield cultivation, and unenclosed rough pasture' [151: *130*]. It can be seen as a modest but vital achievement before the main thrust of enclosure in the eighteenth century [150: *100–10*, *113–33*; 151].

The legal process involved in Scottish enclosures was different from that in England and Wales, and what was enclosed was also different [see 130: *90–1*; on Scottish field systems see 128; 148]. In both cases a statutory process was formed with the Scottish one in some ways a precursor of the Westminster General Acts of the mid-nineteenth century [150: *100–10*; 144: *454–5*; 146]. From 1661 to the end of the century a series of acts was passed to promote agrarian reforms and innovations. The first, in 1661, was a general enclosure act obliging, in principle at least, every proprietor whose lands were worth at least £1000 Scots in annual rent to enclose a minimum of 4 acres per annum for ten years. Smaller landowners were obliged to enclose proportionately smaller areas. The wording of the act is sufficiently ambiguous to raise doubts over its effectiveness. Was it a device which helped reafforestation as much as it improved animal and crop husbandry? In 1669 two further acts built upon the 1661 legislation, and in 1685 the 1661 enclosure act was renewed [150: *100–6*]. These acts have been associated with promoting tree plantations and the expansion of the cattle trade because they were largely used for facilitating, encouraging and protecting enclosures for young trees and grazings. The association of planting timber with enclosure continued in some areas until the late eighteenth century [142: *xix–xx*]. Scottish enclosures well into the eighteenth century were mostly for these purposes of creating *physical boundaries*, for whatever reason, as distinct from the *division* of holdings or the introduction of individual farming over collective husbandry [132: *56*; on grazing aspects see 143].

However, two acts passed in 1695 were quite different. The first, an Act anent Lands lying Runrig, empowered the division of proprietary runrig [126: *127–34*]. The second, the Division of the Commonties Act, empowered the Court of Session to divide waste or uncultivated land which was used as pasture among those proprietors who held commonable rights over them, on the application of a single heritor with interest in the common [133: *191*; 150: *106*]. The origin and evolution of runrig is complicated [146: esp. *69*; see also 127; 128: esp. *70–6*], but for simplicity perhaps it can be likened to the relationship between strip scattering and ownership and tenantry units in the English open fields. But it would be wrong to assume that the act for the division and removal of runrig was the same as the English enclosure act because no provisions were made in the Scottish case for the construction of boundaries for the newly divided holdings. In this sense the 1695 act removed runrig as an impediment to enclosure, and opened up the possibility of enclosure [126: *129*; 132: *57*]. Perhaps the desire for enclosure hastened the end of runrig [146: *71*], because the disappearance of runrig and subsequent enclosure often went together. This seems to have been the case in the eighteenth century in the Lowlands, and it continued into the nineteenth century in the Highlands [133: *192–3*].

The minimum effects of the 1695 acts have been described as a prerequisite to improvement, which 'had been widely though not universally, taken advantage of in the Lowlands by 1770' [134: *17*]. But these late seventeenth-century acts have been seriously questioned as great enclosing devices. They may have had little effect until economic circumstances became favourable, and that may not have been until after 1750 [121: *199*]. Besides, it should be noted that both these acts affected estates only where ownership was intermingled whereas in Scotland the most normal pattern was for ownership to be concentrated in the hands of a single landowner, in which the termination of runrig and the enclosure of commons and open fields could proceed by fiat, without any regard to the position of the tenantry, both before and after the legislation of 1695 [on the abuse of tenantry rights see 133: *191–2*].

Can we measure the extent of enclosure in Scotland? In the mid-eighteenth century a land survey was established, the Military Survey of 1747–55. The resulting work is popularly known as 'Roy's Map', and from its disparate sections O'Dell has reconstructed mainland Scotland. In 1754 there was much farmland apparently enclosed along the eastern coastal belt, along and either side of the Forth–Clyde axis, in the eastern borders [for which see 126: *132–3* and the mid-eighteenth-century concentration of the removal of proprietary runrig] and along the Solway Firth towards Stranraer [137: *61*]. In the Lothians and Berwickshire the system of runrig and commonality of property had already been widely replaced by compact holdings and exclusive possession by 1760 [134: *17–18*]. In spite of these widespread 'enclosures', the composite distribution of open field with enclosed farmland for the same period and even in the same areas shows that in a wider spatial sense the enclosure of mainland Scotland was still awaited in the mid-eighteenth century. 'Roy's Map' perfectly identified the pioneering areas of agrarian reform, but the greatest enclosure movement was yet to come [137: *60*; 134: *19–28*]. In Perthshire in the 1790s at least three-fifths of the arable was unenclosed, a third of Dunbartonshire was open and by 1810 Kincardinshire in general remained open [134: *22–3*; for Argyllshire see 129]. The Montgomery Act of 1770 (10 Geo.III, c.51) encouraged the improvement of land in Scotland held under settlement of strict entail (about one-third of the country was so entailed) [134: *37 et seq*; 133: *202–3*]. It was another example, comparable to the enactments of the second half of the seventeenth century, where the law intervened in a general way to assist and encourage Scottish agricultural improvement, but not necessarily a great enclosing device, which was the hallmark of the English local private act [see also 145: *89*].

The chronology has also been measured, in so far as this is possible. The measuring rod is the registration of commonty divisions from the summons issued in the Court of Session under the aegis of the second 1695 act. The commonties were the lands 'possessed in common by different proprietors' [5: *vii*; 120: *esp. 16*]. There was a peak of activity from 1750–80, especially in the 1760s, and lesser peaks in the 1810s and 1830s. Some authorities emphasise the prices and profit inflation of the Napoleonic wars as the focal point of the general enclosure movement in Scotland, but even by the end of the war much remained open and unenclosed (in the sense of unfenced or unwalled) whilst in fact divided or appropriated in severalty [133: *200*]. Here again the Scottish distinction between *enclosures* and *division* is well made.

Over 650,000 acres of commonty were divided by the Court of Session between 1720–1850, an area equivalent to the size of Warwickshire [119: *252*; 5: *vii*; revised in 121: *199, 203*]. Such an area does not compare with English enclosures but it must be remembered both that some commons lying within the domain of a single landowner will have been enclosed without the intervention of the Court of Sessions, and the amount of land available to agriculture, or at least to enclosed farms, was and is relatively small in Scotland.

Enclosure was often the final deed in a long-drawn-out process of change. The development of large compact farms sometimes preceded the formal enclosure created by rigid boundaries in much the same way as consolidation took place in the English open fields [in general see 133: *190–8*; on the division of runrig without enclosure see 145: esp. *83–9*]. Even in an advanced area like Fife there was land still unenclosed in 1830 that had been in a relatively compact state for 50 years [131: *114*]. In Aberdeenshire, while enclosure of the open fields was over by the 1840s [125: *22*], reclamation of wastes, which in England would often be referred to as enclosure, was still taking place into the 1850s [ibid.: *56–7, 195–6*].

Though this pamphlet is mainly concerned with parliamentary enclosure it is necessary to mention other forms of enclosure in order to put the scale of what we are considering into perspective. Kerridge believes that historians have overestimated the importance of parliamentary enclosure. By about 1700 he suggests that only 'one-quarter of the enclosure of England and Wales remained to be undertaken' thus relegating to limbo 'the hoary fable of the supreme importance of parliamentary enclosure' [69: 24]. It is not merely that parliamentary enclosure diverts attention from his own views of the origin and progress of agricultural revolution but also he wishes to reduce the importance of all enclosures, seeking other changes as the heart of agrarian reform. Earlier summaries in this chapter suggest that 21 per cent of England was enclosed by act, which, if Kerridge is correct in his own appraisal of the survival of open fields and commons, does not leave much margin for enclosure by private agreement during the eighteenth and nineteenth centuries. Either Kerridge's estimate of the amount of land available for future enclosure in 1700 is too low or other authorities have overstated the case of non-parliamentary enclosure after 1700. McCloskey, for example, says that in 1700 an open field system of some sort or other existed in a 'broad swath' across England but that 150 years later '5,000 odd acts of Parliament *and at least an equal number of voluntary agreements* had swept it away' [72: *15*, my emphasis; see also 73: *123–5*]. He also states that one-half of the agricultural land of England was enclosed during the eighteenth and nineteenth centuries. The evidence is taken from Ernle and Slater, giving a guess by Slater of about 8 million acres enclosed by private agreement against 6 million acres by parliamentary act. The 6 million acres is not seriously disputed though it should be reckoned nearer to 7 million. The 8 million acres is now completely unsupportable. Chambers and Mingay are more cautious: 'It is impossible to say how much land was enclosed by agreement rather than by Act, but it must have been very large, perhaps half as great as the open field area enclosed by Act' [46: *78*], which would give a total area enclosed of something like 9–10 million acres. This is more plausible simply in terms of the finite area of land available.

Kerridge and McCloskey have therefore identified the two areas of debate: was parliamentary enclosure so important when compared with pre-eighteenth-century enclosure, and was parliamentary enclosure so important when set against the volume of private enclosure in the eighteenth and nineteenth centuries?

Historians of post-Tudor England have suggested that evidence of anti-enclosure committees, pamphleteers and depopulation enquiries, as well as known enclosure agreements, undermine the scale and importance of the later parliamentary enclosures. But was the weight of words in public outcry and public enquiry inversely proportional to the number of acres affected? As Darby points out

> it may seem strange to find that, after all, the Midlands were the main area of Parliamentary enclosure. The counties which had produced such a volume of complaint in Tudor times were the very ones in which open fields flourished triumphantly right on into the eighteenth and even into the nineteenth century. How is the paradox to be explained? [55: *322*]

Much of England outside the Midlands was already enclosed before the fifteenth or sixteenth centuries or had never been 'open'. The political message that was broadcast may have distorted the magnitude of the events.

A recent survey of the period 1600–1750 suggests that perhaps Kerridge had a valid point in emphasising pre-parliamentary enclosure [42: *66*]. Renewed authority has now been given to the 1607 Depopulation Inquisition as a source for sixteenth-century enclosures, a source incidentally in which Kerridge had little faith; and if that inquiry is more acceptable, then perhaps so are those of the sixteenth century [81]. The enclosures evidence from the Decree Rolls adds weight to the argument. Beresford's use of this source confirms our impressions about Leicestershire, Warwickshire, Lincolnshire and Northamptonshire as counties affected by seventeenth-century anti-enclosure action and which we know had a history of enclosure immediately prior to mass enclosure by act after c.1750 [38]. For example, at least 25 per cent of Leicestershire was enclosed before 1607. By 1710 the proportion was 47 per cent [42: *69*]. With the new evidence we might consider raising this figure. But we also know that 47 per cent of Leicestershire was enclosed by act of parliament after 1730, so if we revise pre-parliamentary enclosure estimates upwards we are virtually dismissing any possibility of enclosures by agreement in any significant numbers in the eighteenth and nineteenth centuries [107: *180*]. Very few other attempts have been made to estimate the chronological history of enclosure for any large areas like counties, but in so far as it has been done it reveals considerable gaps in information. For example, in Durham, Hodgson can account for 29 per cent of the county enclosed in two phases c.1550–1730 (peaking in the 1630s) and 1750–1870 (peaking during the two classic phases of parliamentary enclosure in the 1760s and the 1810s); 15 per cent was never enclosed at all; leaving 56 per cent to be accounted for by medieval enclosure or by private agreement that has left no documentary trace [63].

To summarise, perhaps the best that we can say with current information is that enclosures in the 200 years before 1700 were probably more important than was once believed, but if that is so then enclosure by agreement was probably rather limited after that date. Parliamentary enclosure, if not the most dominant form of enclosure ever known in England was, nevertheless, the most important after 1700.

3   Enclosure and Investment: The Decision to Enclose

(i) GENERAL FACTORS

IT would be easy to catalogue the types of economic factors which may have motivated capital investment in agriculture. We could analyse changes in aggregate demand by investigating population growth, by investigating relative price movements, by looking at the supply of funds to finance capital projects, by looking at technical changes and the relationships with soil and topography, and so on. Such a catalogue might be more baffling than revealing. What is really required is to distinguish the causes from the favourable conditions, in which case it might be a question of conjunction of factors rather than prime causes [66: *272*].

In Warwickshire, Martin identified a conversion of arable to pasture after 1750 resulting from enclosure, perhaps in response to the long period of depressed prices in arable farming in the preceding three decades. Then up to 1780 enclosure was encouraged by a reversal of the price trend and the long upward movement of food prices. In this case enclosure perhaps was followed by improvements in arable production rather than a land use change. The phase after 1780 can be related to the influence from a growing food market and sharply rising land prices [77: *24–9*]. In the Scottish Lowlands 'enclosure was *normally* accompanied by an expansion of arable and mixed farming, not by the laying down of plough to grass and houses to cattlesheds: land was also reclaimed in many areas from the waste and the moor' [141: *328*, my emphasis]. The enclosure of common and waste in the north Somerset uplands in the 1770s may have been the response to the upward trend of wheat prices after 1750 because the lighter soils were more easily adapted to tillage under conditions of enhanced revenue. The richer but heavier soils of the wet grasslands in the county were not enclosed until the war years, perhaps a response to the rise in meat prices. In this second case it was the organisation of existing grazing lands which changed rather than the land use [39]. In the one case relative price movements may have

36

hastened enclosure and in the other the overstocking of commons was alleviated by upgrading the productivity of the wastes [114: *101*].

These few examples indicate the approaches that have been made to answer the broad question of why there was so much parliamentary enclosure. The problem is that we may confuse observable outcomes with investment motives. If the two are the same then enclosure might be heralded as an unqualified entrepreneurial success, but we must remain cautious at this early stage in the investigation.

(ii) The open fields: inflexible or adaptable?

McCloskey reminds us that the antithesis of 'why' enclosure after 1750 is why were conditions, catalysts or motives not right before 1750: 'So plain has the inefficiency [of the open fields] seemed that the question has been not why enclosure occurred when it did, by why it did not occur earlier' [72: *17*; see also 32: *64*]. His later work on the open fields, on strip division and scattering of strips in the open fields which he hypothesised as an insurance against the risks of agricultural failure, suggests there were considerable reasons why the open fields persisted [73–5]. There is a protracted debate, that has reached no consensus, over the organisation and dynamic of the English open fields, involving discussion of the scattering and dispersion of holdings for the purposes of risk aversion within the theoretical framework of property rights analysis. It is tangential to the substance of this pamphlet and though the protagonists involved are not all itemised in the bibliography the reader is advised nevertheless to consult the pages of *The Journal of Economic History, Explorations in Economic History, The Journal of European Economic History* and *The Journal of Development Economics*, among others, for the late 1970s [see also 54].

The disjunction of factors before 1750 is just as important as their conjunction after, but the inefficiency of the open fields is by no means as plain and obvious as once it seemed. The retarding qualities historically attributed to them have been refuted in varying degrees in a number of studies. Kerridge suggested that an outstanding feature of common-field husbandry was the liberty the cultivator had to choose what crops he liked in the various parts of the particular open field, though within a set field course. He also suggested that this was nothing new and not necessarily indicative of progress or adaptability [69: *94–5*]. Havinden demonstrated from parish agreements the way the open fields were regulated to meet changing economic circumstances, in which case enclosure was perhaps rendered unnecessary [62]. A counter-argument has been developed from similar parish agreements, using them to indicate the constraints and retarding qualities of open field practice [107: *ch.6*; and on the general debate see also 77: *21–2*; 29; 118: *163–70*].

The inefficiencies of the open fields, though not satisfactorily refuted or vindicated in these counter-arguments, are nevertheless subject to irrefutable qualifications. The open fields were not completely backward or obstructive but neither did they permit complete autonomy in decision-making [on a general theory of rigidity in the open fields see 74: *151–2*]. A case in point might have been a leading landowner in the Derbyshire village of Mapleton whose lands in the six open fields in the 1720s were scattered in 75 separate pieces. The enclosure of 1731 consolidated his ownership into one field by exchanging his lands in the other five with like-minded neighbours [58].

It is, however, by no means certain that enclosure automatically reduced the technical inefficiencies of all agriculturalists. In parts of Durham, for example, agriculture remained technically backward after enclosure and made more widespread the orthodox technique of two crops and a fallow [63: esp. *96–8*]. As Thomas Davis recognised in 1811, 'severalty makes a good farmer better' but it makes 'a bad one worse' [12: *46*].

Even if crop choice within the open fields is evidence of flexibility, it has yet to be demonstrated as a widespread practice. Furthermore, inflexibility was most evident in some areas by the frustrated desire to adjust cropping to withstand a heavier animal population. The inflexibility was not so much within arable farming as in limiting choice between arable and pastoral or mixed farming. The pressures upon common grazing in Buckinghamshire, for example, created by the undesirable but unavoidable practice of overstocking animals, resulted in bottlenecks in the local economy once the desire to increase pastoral farming at the expense of arable farming gained momentum. Adjustments in local field and stinting rules inhibited this desire and halted the expansion of animal activities, or even reduced existing ones. Shortage of land for pastoral activities seems to have developed as a result, protracted for a century or more before 1750 [107: *ch.6*; and for sixteenth- and seventeenth-century evidence of pasture shortages in Kesteven see 82: *93*]. The problem may have come to a head in the two or three decades before 1750 during a depression of arable prices when real incomes improved and increased the demand for animal products [for a summary and fresh interpretation of the agricultural depression of 1730–50 see 35]. There is considerable evidence in this period to suggest conversion to grass, with enclosure as one of the agents of change. The early acts before 1750 may have been an alternative to the traditional Chancery instruments of the seventeenth century, an extension of enclosure activity stretching back to the fifteenth century in which conversion to grass was usual. This was the case for much of Warwickshire, Leicestershire and the Midland heartland generally [77: *27*; 66: *266*]. It is not difficult to see a connection with long-run economic trends because these counties of early parliamentary enclosure are the same counties involved in the 1607 and earlier depopulation enquiries. Throughout the seventeenth century and well on into the third quarter of the eighteenth, central England came to look greener than ever [55: *326*]. Even Durham, a county not usually associated with the heavier soils of the Midlands, also experienced a wave of early enclosures (pre-1750) and these were related to the development or extension of the pastoral economy [63: *93*].

In Lindsey it appears that pre-eighteenth-century enclosure took place on water-retentive soils and marshlands associated with reclamation, and this enclosure arose from the desire to increase or improve pastoral activity. But such a move did not act as a spur to dissolve the open arable fields or other features of communal life; instead the general concentration on grass farming served to keep arable farming in a backward state, the open fields surviving well into the eighteenth and on into the nineteenth centuries. In this case pastoralism caused the enclosure of the arable to be delayed [68: esp. *139*].

(iii) Productivity gains and enclosure

Contemporaries were generally certain about the productivity gains achieved by enclosure. In the Vale of Aylesbury, for example, Arthur Young reported that 'the tenants reap bushels, where they ought to have quarters'. After enclosure the productivity gains for landlords were just as impressive, 'the rents before were fourteen shillings but now arable lands let to twenty eight shillings per acre; none under a guinea; and grass from forty shillings to three pounds, all tithe free. This rise of rents on enclosing justifies by observation on the expediency of inclosing' [16: *24–5*]. It is interesting that Young linked productivity effects for both farmers and landlords together (improved output and improved rent) [on productivity effects see 86: *102–12*; 17: *91*; and on the problems of relating landlords' profit through rental changes and farmers' profit through productivity gains see 118: *211*]. It may also be the case that farmers' profits were enhanced after enclosure not necessarily through a simple improvement in output, but also, or instead, by a reduction in expenses, in spite of increased rents [for an illustration of this see ibid.: *212–13*].

Enclosure petitions, bills and acts complained of the unimprovable nature of the soil while husbandry remained in open fields, dispersed in small pieces, with intermixed ownership and tenancy, adding that open fields were capable of considerable improvement if divided and allotted among the proprietors in severalty. A preamble to this effect headed most major enclosure documents, though it might have meant little more than the country solicitor using existing petitions, bills and acts to frame succeeding ones. There is, though, a good deal of evidence from modern scholarship to support the idea of productivity gains at enclosure, though not always on a dramatic scale. In some Oxfordshire parishes there was a 10 per cent improvement in the yields of the basic grains when enclosed fields were compared with open ones [158: *479*], and in both Northamptonshire and Warwickshire there were similar improvements [107: *95–7*]. For a large number of widely scattered places both Yelling and Turner have demonstrated considerable improvements in grain yields when comparing enclosed villages with open field ones, improvements of the order of 25 per cent [110: *497–500*; 118: *171–2, 203–4*].

The main problem with productivity studies of this kind is that they are not necessarily comparisons of the same parishes before and after enclosure, but rather of open field parishes and enclosed ones co-existing at the same time. The ones with inherently more fertile soils may be already enclosed, or the gains may not be from enclosure alone but from better practice techniques, including the freedom of crop choice which was so problematic in the open fields. So at Barton upon Humber in Lincolnshire in 1801 there was 'a decrease in the number of acres under the plough since the inclosure of 1793, *yet from a superior mode* of cultivation' there was 'an increase upon the whole', a view which was echoed in other Lincolnshire parishes. But enclosure by itself could produce gains by eliminating losses through trespass and too frequent fallows. In Standish in Gloucestershire two crops and a fallow held back the productivity of the open fields whereas if enclosed 'they would not require a fallow oftener than once in six or seven years'; in Bosbury in Herefordshire the common fields were 'highly injurious to agriculture, as they invariably lie fallow every third year'; and in Latton in Wiltshire the open fields lay fallow every fourth year: 'The course of common field husbandry allows not of turnipping nor of any other late and valuable improvements in agriculture' [110: vol. 190: *102*; vol. 189: *193, 225*; vol. 195: *85* respectively]. Enclosure was the vehicle for improvement but in itself was not inherently an improvement.

Enclosure often brought about land use changes. In the Midland clays there was a move out of arable into pasture up to the late eighteenth century. In Worcestershire there was an increase in wheat cultivation at the expense of the other grains and a general improvement in the variety of crop combinations and rotations [117: esp. *24–34*]. How do we measure productivity changes which arise from land use alterations? The answer might be through farm revenues, and in the absence of data on farmers' incomes these can perhaps be inferred from rental changes.

(iv) RENT AND PRODUCTIVITY GAINS

It has been suggested that from a landlord's point of view enclosure was an investment, the profit from which was a higher rent. If rents doubled after enclosure, which was not unusual, net profit could be of the order of 15–20 per cent, making enclosure one of the best investments of the age. On the Fitzwilliam estates there was a 16 per cent return in original outlay after enclosure; on certain Lincolnshire estates in the 1760s there was a 32 per cent per annum improvement on the rent roll attributable to enclosure [cited in 108: *245–7*]. There is some confusion over gross and net measurements of return, nevertheless the pattern is clear enough, with considerable supporting evidence of higher rents in enclosed situations compared with open ones [for examples from Lincolnshire, Oxfordshire, Buckinghamshire and Warwickshire see 34: *90–3*; 17: *91–4;* 157: *359–60*; 77: *29*].

No doubt rental revaluation was important in the decision to enclose but unfortunately it has been treated as an automatic economic gain rather than as one element leading to considered economic or entrepreneurial decisions. Purdum, however, has set up a descriptive model of the responsiveness of landlords to monetary benefits [87]. If the efficiency gain of enclosed over open fields is measured by rental changes then enclosure was easily financed by these rental improvements. There is the hint of cost benefit when Purdum introduces the idea of discovering what factors influencing gains from enclosure 'were known prior to enclosure', because such factors may have influenced the timing of enclosure. For the owner of a single estate such prior knowledge was probably only guesswork or based on information from neighbours, but for the owner of more than one estate the potential to predict future rates of return based on existing experience may have been crucial in the timing of enclosure. The main finding to emerge is that rent as the monetary return from enclosure must be measured for efficiency gain against the rates of return on alternative investments. The model is therefore couched in terms of opportunity costs [see also 72]. For example, if rent returns were less than the prevailing rate of usury of 5 per cent then rental gains as a motive for parting with investment funds cannot be accepted as a working hypothesis and enclosure therefore was an inefficient use of capital. Purdum's rates on five manors out of five investigated in Nottinghamshire exceeded 5 per cent.

But what about changes in interest rates and what about alternative investments? Ashton and McCloskey regarded interest rate movements as the prime economic indicator which at times encouraged enclosures and at others held them in abeyance [31; 72]. But Purdum considers that if enclosures were as profitable as was popularly believed then movements in interest rates would have had only a minimal effect on the decision to enclose. Certainly his rates of return support that view, but this was at an opportunity cost of only 5 per cent. In the mid-eighteenth-century Levant trade one merchant considered that the risks were not worth while unless an annual return of 8 per cent could be assured, meaning a gross profit of 30 to 40 per cent over four years, which was the gestation period of the original outlay [R. Davis, *Aleppo and Devonshire Square: English Traders in the Levant in the Eighteenth Century* (1967), *222, 226*]. While trade and enclosures are not comparable, a gestation period is also appropriate in other forms of investment. This is a significant gap in our literature of the eighteenth century.

Rental improvements have been related to the theory of property rights. A spectrum of property rights existed with common ownership at one end and private ownership at the other. The former was the ultimate in shared or non-exclusive rights and the latter was an exclusive right in property. Between the two existed a combination of rights: some were temporary common rights in force during periods of fallow; some were full common rights operating for long periods on commons and open fields; and some were partial common rights where partial or piecemeal enclosures existed. Furthermore, these rights could vary through the course of the harvest year. The more exclusive the right the greater the opportunity for rent maximisation, the less exclusive the right the more dissipated the rent because more people had to share it. The ability to gain exclusivity of property ownership may have been reflected in the extent of improved post-enclosure rents [32: esp. *64–5*; see also 33; 54: *ch.3*]. Thus it has been argued that Tudor enclosures, in so far as they were primarily for extending pastoral husbandry, had the most to gain from renegotiated rents at enclosure because grazing rights were the least exclusive property rights available. The argument then follows that parliamentary enclosure, which was essentially in arable areas the ownership of which was already more exclusive, therefore commanded a lower level of rent gain. Consequently these enclosures occurred later because the gains were smaller. The proposition, while interesting, is far too simplistic, misunderstands Tudor enclosures which were not simply to separate grazing rights but rather to enclose arable fields and convert to pasture, and does not accommodate the great variability that there was in enclosures, many of which were composite land reforms or involved changes of land use.

Allen offers two explanations for the rise of rents after enclosure. Firstly, farmers of enclosed farms could pay more because of post-enclosure efficiency gains, though alternatively enclosure could have led to a redistribution of income from farmers to landlords if open field farms were underrented in the first place. This second explanation rests on the outcome of clauses in enclosure acts which terminated existing leases. The opportunity was given, effectively, to abandon these leases in the mid-term and allow landlords and tenants to renegotiate them, though if necessary with compensation for those leases with less than 21 years to run [10: *37*]. Yelling asks the question, what happened when enclosures took place in times of inflation? 'There is some reason to believe that rent levels tended to freeze in the immediate pre-enclosure period, and to be released in the re-negotiation of rents and leases on enclosure' [118: *211*]. This is precisely the issue which Allen has tried to unscramble. The period from the mid-eighteenth century to the end of the Napoleonic wars was one of rising prices and thus any Ricardian rent surpluses arising from this rise in prices of agricultural produce on open field estates would have accrued to the tenants because their rents were fixed, and not to the landlords who thus would have fixed money incomes. Enclosure, it is supposed, allowed landlords to recoup these surpluses by exacting new rents now corrected for inflation. Allen's research supports this proposition to the extent that he calculates that only about one-half of the open field surpluses accrued to the landlords as rent or to the church and state in tithes and taxes. While it is plausible that rents lagged behind inflation, especially the inflation of the Napoleonic war years, the rate of inflation before 1790, a period which encompassed the entire first phase of parliamentary enclosure, was not very pronounced. But crucially, Allen's theory is based on data from Arthur Young from the 1760s, a period of only modest price inflation. In addition, it is hard to maintain confidence in Young when we learn from Allen that grain yields were actually smaller, on average by 9, 18 and 12 per cent respectively for wheat, barley and oats when comparing enclosed fields with open ones [29: *949*, my percentage differences based on Allen's mean yields figures], a conclusion which goes against the findings of most modern scholarship, including my own, which supports the idea of productivity gains [as in 109: *497–500*; 118: *171–2, 203–4*; 158: *479*]. At the moment therefore the evidence favours the alternative explanation to Allen's, namely productivity gains at enclosure, part of which accrued to the landlord in terms of higher rents. The exact nature of the division of productivity gains between landlords and tenants is clearly debatable at the present state of research, perhaps Yelling has summarised the nearest to a consensus in saying that the farmers are believed to have benefited, though to a lesser extent [118: *211*].

(v) COST-BENEFIT

Let us return to a point raised in the previous section. We cannot discuss profitability and productivity without establishing what the enclosers expected to gain from their investments. Were accountancy procedures, however crude, employed? As historians we are wont to analyse the outcome of enclosure in terms of cost-benefit, but did the encloser also view his investment in this way?

Purdum's rental analysis rests heavily on an interpretation of opportunity costs, as do those arguments which seek a relationship between chronology of enclosure and movements in the rate of interest, in which the rate of usury is the assumed opportunity cost [eg. 72; 74: *136–7*]. This question of opportunity costs must be taken further and must not be ignored in examples where enclosure was *not* financed out of borrowed capital. As McCloskey points out, those who ignore interest rates on the grounds that much enclosure was financed out of current income and not by mortgage miss the significance of opportunity costs. To expend current income on enclosures certainly avoided future interest repayments on loans, but incurred the penalty of the foregone income by not investing in alternative projects whose rate of return exceeded the rate of usury, usually measured as the yield on consols. Self-financing therefore also carried an element of opportunity cost [74: *137*]. Some evidence suggests that enclosers were sensitive to opportunity costs, invoking the capital cost of enclosure only in terms of the foregone income from investing the same money elsewhere. At Hessle in the East Riding in the 1790s, for example, it was calculated that the opportunity cost of the enclosure was 2 shillings per acre. The expected improvement in rent from 20 to 30 shillings per acre greatly exceeded the foregone income from alternative investment. The principal landowner in the Buckinghamshire hamlet of Sedrup in 1775 calculated the expected improvement on his estate in the event of an enclosure. Current rents were £404–15–0 and improved rents would be £689–5–6 (including some old enclosures and orchards); but the net improvement would not be £284–10–6 (i.e. new minus old rents), but rather £232–0–6, which allowed for a deduction of £30 for the improvement of the tithes, and a second deduction of £22–10–0, the foregone income from laying out £560 on enclosure costs at 4½ per cent interest [Buckinghamshire County Record Office, D/LE/8/100]. Enclosure costs were considered only in terms of an opportunity cost. The projected rent improvement would have repaid the capital cost after three years.

Such an example of cost-benefit, while not commonplace, was also not so unusual. For example, it was not unusual for recognised enclosure commissioners and land surveyors to make this kind of estimate as a preliminary to framing a bill [104: esp. *41*]. Perhaps the importance of opportunity costs was greater and more widespread than scholarship has allowed. Sir William Lee of Hartwell in Buckinghamshire valued an estate in nearby Bishopstone at a little over £1554 (date unknown but probably in the 1770s). Bearing in mind the interest such a sum would earn if invested, Sir William was advised not to offer more than £1400, thus allowing for the foregone income in such investment [Buckinghamshire County Record Office, D/LE/8/4]. In this case, on a one-year basis, he was allowing for a 10 per cent return for foregone income, though this is not stated in the document.

(vi) OTHER ECONOMIC CONSIDERATIONS

Before discussing obvious economic factors, we should bear in mind that relatively irrational factors may have influenced the timing of enclosure. For example, lack of entrepreneurship coupled with agricultural conservatism is sometimes alleged to have produced late enclosures. In Kesteven 'poor farmers and a conservative tradition failed to help, if they did not positively hold back, parliamentary enclosure' [82: *94*]. In neighbouring Lindsey the backwardness of the arable farmer, tenurial bottlenecks, and local conservatism, rather than fundamental physical environmental factors, are said to have partly determined the late arrival of enclosure on the lighter soils of the region [68: *147*]. Thomas Stone in 1787 pointed to the conservatism of the open field farmer who through centuries of inheritance believed that he already farmed by best practice methods and who, given a village and farms newly enclosed, might have looked for another open field situation 'rather than subject himself to deviate in the least from the beaten track of his ancestors for the means of subsistence' [15: *25*]. Who is to say that the landlords through their own perceptions of custom and change may not have been conservative as well, and held enclosure in abeyance?

But there are more concrete economic reasons why enclosure may have been delayed and why the whole movement was protracted over time. The cost of enclosure for most owners was a serious issue, a dividing line between financial independence and a lesser position in the social and agricultural hierarchy. A consideration of costs could hold enclosure in abeyance, whether by the individual or by the collective decision of those in the same socio-economic niche. We must also consider more general factors about the economy and society at large in which enclosures were situated. It becomes a question not merely why enclosure was not completed by 1750 but also why it was concentrated in two relatively restricted peaks of activity within the broader chronology of 1750–1830.

Whether or not a landowner could afford to enclose depended on the availability of funds and their cost, that is the rate of interest. Whether he wanted to enclose also depended on his judgement of the tenants' ability to pay higher rents after enclosure, in which case he needed to be sensitive to tenants' income, and the price trends which affected that income.

Were interest rates or prices the more potent factor? Considering prices first, the first graph on Figure 4 shows a money or current wheat price index for the period 1731–1819, with a rise in prices up to the early 1790s [see 107: *112–13*]. When the peaks and troughs are smoothed this increase settled down gently at 1–2 per cent per annum. Thereafter the price rise was dramatic with wild fluctuations and also a much steeper rate of inflation which when smoothed advanced annually by up to 10 per cent and more, and in outstanding years by 100 per cent or more. The 'Agricultural Depression' of 1730–50 is evident, when though prices may not have actually fallen they did remain relatively static. The beginning of the rise in wheat prices therefore came a little after the mid-century. The coincidence of this price history with the rate of enclosure activity is clear; the permanent turning point in prices coinciding with the emergence of significant numbers of parliamentary enclosures, and the major peak of enclosure during the Napoleonic wars coinciding with a 300–500 per cent increase in money prices when compared with the 1730s. Hunt, working on Leicestershire, advanced an explanation of enclosure based on this price trend at least up to 1795. Thereafter there was little enclosure in that county though he suggested a relationship between the high wartime prices and the enclosure of common and waste in other Midland counties [66; esp. *266–7*]. Williams similarly explains the incidence of wartime enclosures in Somerset where for him the lower prices in the post-war depression account for the subsequent fall-off in enclosure activity [114: *101*]. Yelling refers to the 'greatest amount of enclosure' which 'of course coincided with the great upsurge in the price of agricultural products which occurred during the French wars', and for marginal lands 'it needed the high prices of the Napoleonic war period to encourage conversion' [118: *16, 34*]. Chambers and Mingay also champion a prices approach to explain the chronology of enclosure [46: *84*]. A matter which may have confused the reader is that the identifiable turning point in prices around 1750 precedes the main thrust of the first enclosure movement in the 1760s and 70s by 10 years or more. Contemporaries, of course, could not conceivably recognise a permanent point until

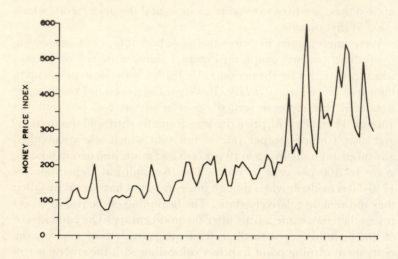

Figure 4   Trends in Wheat Prices and Interest Rates 1731–1819

Sources: Taken from M. E. Turner, *English Parliamentary Enclosure* (1980), *107, 112–13*.

The *Money Price Index* is taken from B. R. Mitchell, *Abstract of British Historical Statistics* (1962), *486–7*, who reports in shillings per bushel the price of *wheat* at Exeter, Eton and Winchester. The price series used here is the Winchester one recalculated as an index with base 100 in 1701. This date is chosen to fit in with the base dates used in other indexes itemised below.

The *Real Price Index* is the money index above deflated by the Schumpeter–Gilboy price index of consumer goods other than cereals as printed in Mitchell, *468–9*, thus

[*continued*]

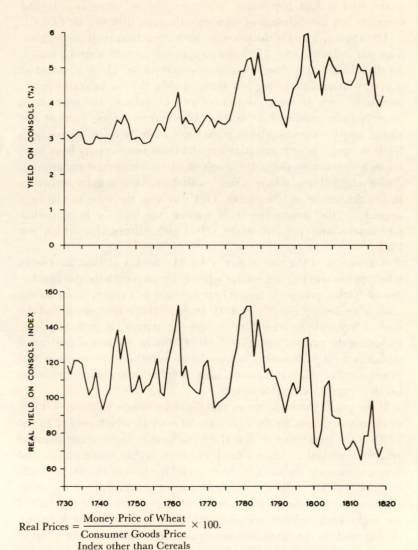

$$\text{Real Prices} = \frac{\text{Money Price of Wheat}}{\substack{\text{Consumer Goods Price} \\ \text{Index other than Cereals}}} \times 100.$$

The *Yield on Consols* is taken from S. Homer, *A History of Interest Rates* (1963), *161, 195*.

The *Real Yield on Consols* is the ordinary yield itemised above, indexed on the same base date as the other indexes employed, and then deflated by the Schumpeter–Gilboy consumer goods index as printed in Mitchell, *468–9*, thus

$$\text{Real Yield on Consols} = \frac{\text{Yield on Consols Index}}{\substack{\text{Consumer Goods Price} \\ \text{Index}}} \times 100.$$

years after it had happened. What we see therefore is a lagged response [on the diffusion of enclosure through time see 51: *242–3*].

The attractiveness of the price theory is clear in at least one respect. The war inflation, after 1793, does appear to provide a strong reason for the additional enclosure of common and waste. Though such land was poor in quality, giving low arable yields, the rise in arable prices may have been an incentive to enclose and reclaim, and possibly to convert from grazing into arable. The higher prices, even at low yields, may have given returns in excess of what they would have been if left as common or rough pasture, and these returns may have been enough to warrant the costs involved in enclosing and reclaiming. Again a lagged response is evident with the peak of activity occurring in the decade or so after 1800. This was also the time of vigorous appeal for the improvement of wastes, particularly from parliamentarians and parliamentary select committees [for which see 112].

A criticism of the prices theory by McCloskey is that the rise in wheat prices was less impressive when compared with the rise in other prices. 'Other prices are meant here to stand as a rough proxy for the costs of enclosure' [72: *31*; 74: *151*]. In general it is true to say that the cost of enclosure increased more than the increase in general prices, including the price of wheat [107: *131–4*]. But in real terms, compared with a general price index, though the great inflation of money wheat prices is reduced it is still quite clearly an inflationary price movement [as in Figure 4, real price index].

If the prices theory helps to explain the wartime enclosures it less obviously accounts for the first wave of activity which peaked in the 1770s. One suggestion is that these enclosures came about because enclosers wished to change land use from arable into pasture, and hence to increase the stock of animals and the flow of animal products [107: *ch.6*]. This is directly related to price movements in the sense that it was a response to the agricultural depression of the first half of the eighteenth century and the stability of prices in the long run dating back to the late seventeenth century. The peak of enclosure activity occurred in the wake of this price stability rather than during it. A learning process took place producing a diffusion of enclosure activity from the pre-1750 modest beginnings (which included the adjustment of field rules explained in section ii above) to a peak of enclosing in the 1770s. While adjustments provoked by economic stimuli occur instantaneously in some places, the complete adjustment is lagged over some considerable time as the learning process breaks down local custom and conservatism [on diffusion processes see 51: *242–3*]. These early parliamentary enclosures were not necessarily to lay all arable crops down to grass, but allowed more freedom to mix crops with animals. In this respect we should look for relative increases in animal and animal product prices before 1780 rather than the modest rise in grain prices which actually occurred. Unfortunately a series of animal prices is not available, or at least not one to compare with the series of grain prices.

Ashton focused attention on money supply as a determinant of enclosure investment. The yield on consols was the indication of money demand and supply chosen (as in Figure 4). An observable relationship between the fluctuations in the yield and enclosure activity was identified. Though interest rates rose gently over the course of much of the eighteenth century they were relatively stable or declining in the 1760s and 1770s. Conversely, high interest rates during the American war of the late 1770s and early 1780s coincided with a decline in enclosure activity [31: *40–1*]. So, before 1790 enclosure could apparently be related to the ease or difficulty of borrowing money, falling or stable interest rates encouraging investment in enclosure and rising ones taking funds away from agriculture and other private investment by attracting them into government financing of the American war. At first sight the explanation seems to fall down after 1790 when interest rates reached record eighteenth-century heights and so also did enclosure activity. But as Figure 4 shows, the trend in interest rates failed to keep pace with inflation, and the real rate was generally stable or even falling from about 1750 onwards. The wartime peaks are still evident (Austrian Succession, Seven Years' War, American war), but the 'dearness' of the French war seems to evaporate into a period of 'cheap' or cheapening money [74: *137–8*; see also 51; 72; 107: *ch.5*].

We are still left with the choice between interest rates and prices. The former explanation has its champions [72; 107], as does the latter [46; 51], but neither is convincing as a full explanation of enclosure activity. At the same time we should not expect either of them to be exclusive explanations. The opportunity cost of investment in enclosure can be compared with other forms of investment, as in consols, but the income from investment in enclosure for the landlords came from rents, and these must have reflected price changes in order to maximise income without bankrupting the tenants, and the income from enclosure for the owner-occupiers was a delicate balance between costs (the cost of borrowing for example) and revenue gains which necessarily reflected price movements.

4 Investment and Cost:
Part 1, The Economic Cost

(i) THE TOTAL COST

IN the last section we isolated the motivating forces which may have encouraged landlords and owner-occupiers to invest heavily in enclosures in the eighteenth and nineteenth centuries, particularly the economic factors which may have triggered off such investment and sustained it. The suggestion was that there were economic gains through higher output and revenues on the one hand and enhanced rents on the other. This is a petitioners' or landlords' view of investment which gives little consideration to the perspective of those who did not petition for enclosures and may indeed have counter-petitioned against. To the extent that counter-petitions were often couched in terms of the high costs of enclosure a fairer assessment of costs all round is essential before we proceed to discuss the social consequences of enclosure.

Recent research has suggested that the cost of enclosure was greater than scholars believed even as recently as two or three decades ago [97; 78; 104]. This reassessment has shed new light on the social consequences of enclosures [105; 80], and also found that the financing of enclosure was more problematic than was once assumed [108].

We can distinguish two types of costs involved, the public and the personal costs. The former included the costs involved in local negotiations in preparing and presenting the bill to parliament, the cost of soliciting that bill, the parliamentary fees of obtaining the act, fees and expenses paid to the commissioners, their clerks, surveyors and bankers, and the physical costs of enclosure. These last included the cost of fencing the lands allotted to the tithe owners, the cost of making the new roads, bridlepaths and other rights of way, and the costs incurred for husbandry expenses. To elaborate, the tithe owner was not expected to share any of the costs of commuting tithes from a

53

money payment or payment in kind to a land settlement in lieu thereof. This tithe commutation could be equivalent to one-fifth or one-sixth of all open field land and one-seventh or less of the commons and wastes which were enclosed. The cost of doing this would be redistributed as a burden on all the other landowners and quite clearly could be a sizable extra cost. Not only would the tithe owner not contribute to the general expenses of the enclosure but also his subdivision fences which separated his new land from that of his neighbours would be constructed at public expense. The cost of making the roads and other physical items like drains, but predominantly the roads, was usually the result of the commissioners inviting tenders and contracting the work out. As we shall discover, the roads were very costly. The cost of husbandry evidently mainly involved the grass seed which the commissioners purchased and applied to those fields which came out of crops and were laid down to grass in the normal course of husbandry. An enclosure usually took one or more harvests' seasons to complete and the commissioners were vested with the power to administrate local husbandry, including ploughing, seeding and so forth. The fear was that if left to themselves the farmers would not be efficient in attending to their lands in the open fields because they might be allotted (as owner-occupiers) or succeed (as tenants) to land elsewhere in the parish and therefore not gain the full benefit of their own industry. The commissioners as neutral parties ensured the proper upkeep of the village lands.

The commissioners' fees ranged from one guinea per day in the mid-eighteenth century up to two or more by the nineteenth. The clerical fees (often the clerk was a representative of the same firm of solicitors who carried the bill to parliament) likewise were usually daily assessed, though the surveyors' fees were on a per acre basis. In general therefore the longer the enclosure took to administer the greater was the cost, and the larger the surviving open fields or commons in a parish the greater was the cost of surveying.

The public costs were calculated ostensibly to reflect the size *and* quality of lands which were awarded. The commissioners employed the 'quantity' surveyors to make this calculation and so generally we may be assured that it was done on a unit acre basis. 'Quality' surveyors were also employed to ensure fairness over the different qualities of land in the parish [see 106]. There is a lot of suspicion that acre for acre the smaller owners were treated less than fairly in these calculations [78: *138–9*], though some contemporary opinion and some modern scholarship emphasise the impartiality of the commissioners and their staff in the fulfilment of their duties [see particularly 37].

The commissioners began collecting fees to cover public costs before the completion of their work. The fees therefore reflected expected costs rather than actual ones. Sometimes the fees were overestimated, in which case a refund was given, and sometimes they were underestimated, resulting in second or even third supplementary demands for money. The important point was that the money or 'rate' was payable by the landowners during the course of the enclosure or by a specified time after the commissioners had completed their work. Evidence of the commissioners having difficulties in exacting the fees and threatening to call in the bailiff to distrain for unpaid fees suggests considerable hardship by some landowners in finding the large sums of money required, and more particularly in finding this money before the economic benefits from enclosure could be translated into higher incomes [see particularly 104]. Raising a rate was the most common method the commissioners used to pay for enclosures. In the nineteenth century, however, especially for the enclosure of common and waste, they increasingly allowed the sale of communal land to cover costs, or deducted land from individual owners before allotting; such land, in either case, was sold by private treaty or auction and the proceeds from the sales paid for the public costs of enclosure [in Somerset this was common even in the eighteenth century, for which see 39; see also 47; 108: esp. *240–2*]. The pure financial burden of enclosure was therefore easier to bear, but the amount of land deducted and sold could be as much as half the land available for allotment [39: *122–4*], reducing the final allotments to some owners to uneconomic units or mere gardens.

Such were the public costs and the two methods the commissioners used to collect the appropriate money. The personal costs principally involved the fencing of allotments, but would also include any additional buildings, drains and other general agricultural improvements. Each landowner had to fence, by outward or ring fences as they were known, his allotment from his neighbours. This fencing had to be completed within a time limit prescribed by the commissioners, usually three, six or less frequently nine or more months after the commissioners had finished the administration of the enclosure. As we shall see, the fencing was a very expensive item. These fences, which defined the boundaries of each person's territory, completed the minimum personal expenditure. But to gain the fullest benefit from farming in severalty the landowners would give serious consideration to subdividing their allotments with subdivision fences to create fields of manageable and economic proportions. They would also consider new drains, buildings, etc. But subdivision fences and other improvements were personal choice decisions and not obligatory under the provisions of the individual acts. It is evident that such internal improvements took many years to complete on many estates and were a continuous long-term call on the finances of those estates.

Three types of fencing have therefore been defined: the tithe owners' fencing at public cost; ring or outward fencing at personal but mandatory cost; and subdivision fencing, an optional personal cost.

Scholarship once held the view that 'the average total costs [of enclosure] for the small proprietors amounted to about £3 [per acre]' [85: 23–4, but my brackets]. Though such costs 'might be a heavy burden' they 'were not insuperable' [ibid.], especially when set against the benefits of farming in severalty. Tate concluded similarly, if the small proprietor was driven out of business in the eighteenth century it was not due to the unreasonable expense of enclosure: 'In this, as in several other matters, it appears then that parliamentary enclosure has been saddled with a responsibility which does not properly belong to it' [97: 265]. Two important issues were, however, substantially neglected until the mid-1960s. Up to £3 per acre reflected the public costs of enclosure (as in Table III) but it was a sum net of the costs of fencing and other costs which finally effected the post-enclosure improvement of the land. Secondly, the financing of enclosure has been a neglected issue and only recently has it been seriously researched, with some surprising results [39; 47; 152].

Martin was the first modern scholar to revise our views on the scale and burdens of enclosure costs, suggesting they had been underestimated and also stressing the heavier penalty which fell on smaller and poorer landowners. Generally speaking, unit costs increased the smaller the amount of land awarded, thus defying any notions of equity [78: 114, 138–9; see also 28: 105]. There is also Henry Homer's contemporary comment that fencing costs were larger per unit on progressively smaller allotments, amply confirmed by recent research. For example, for an allotment four times the size of another only twice as much ring fencing was required [13: 97–8; 78: 140; 74: 144–5, 149–50].

Table III

Public Cost of Parliamentary Enclosure in England 1730–1844
(in shillings per acre)

Period[a]	Lincs[b] (Lindsey)	Oxon	Leics	Warws	Wilts	Bucks[c]
Pre-1760		18.0[e]	12.0	11.0	10.3[h]	
1760s	13.0 (16.0)	15.1	12.0	13.7	21.6[i]	16.9 (15.8)
1770s	18.7 (28.1)	21.1	16.0	19.6	25.3	21.2 (18.8)
1780s	20.3 (27.3)[d]	21.3[f]	11.0	19.7	17.4	24.1 (23.9)
1790s	20.3 (22.3)	39.1	23.0	34.1	17.0	39.2 (37.5)
1800–14				58.8[g]	52.8	81.9 (90.6)
1815–44				83.9	43.3	71.7 (71.8)

[a] The date of the act determined which period an enclosure would be counted in.
[b] The first figure is derived from Tate and the bracketed figure from Swales. The latter is total cost divided by the net acreage after deducting tithe, glebe, gravel pits and other areas financed at public cost. The former estimation is the one usually used, that is, total cost divided by gross acreage.
[c] The first figure is the average of all the individual average costs of enclosure. That is to say, the 16.9 shillings per acre in the 1760s is the mean of ten separate average costs. This seems to be the usual method of estimation. The bracketed figure is the total acreage enclosed in the decade divided by the total costs for the decade for those enclosures for which details are available. The estimates can be quite strikingly different.
[d] 3 enclosures only: [e] 1 enclosure only: [f] 3 enclosures only.
[g] 3 enclosures only: [h] 2 enclosures only: [i] 1 enclosure only. In all other cases at least 4 cost estimates were available.

Holderness in 1971 used the information from Lindsey, Oxon, Leics and Warws, which were already published, and added information from other odd enclosure accounts to give national averages for the given periods of 10.5, 12.7, 19.3, 19.2, 31.0, 42.8, and 67.3 shillings per acre respectively [64: *163*].

Sources: T. H. Swales, 'The Parliamentary Enclosures of Lindsey', *Reports and Papers of the Architectural and Archaeological Societies of Lincolnshire and Northamptonshire*, in two parts, XLII (1937), New Series 2 (1938); W. E. Tate, 'The Cost of Parliamentary Enclosure in England', *EcHR*, v (1952); H. G. Hunt, 'The Chronology of Parliamentary Enclosure in Leicestershire', *EcHR*, x (1957–8); J. M. Martin, 'The Cost of Parliamentary Enclosure in Warwickshire', in E. L. Jones (ed.), *Agriculture and Economic Growth in England 1650–1815* (1967); J. R. Ellis, *Parliamentary Enclosure in Wiltshire* (Unpublished PhD, University of Bristol, 1971); M. E. Turner, *Some Social and Economic Considerations of Parliamentary Enclosure in Buckinghamshire 1738–1865* (Unpublished PhD, University of Sheffield, 1973).

Table III brings together for comparative purposes estimates of the public costs per acre of enclosure for various counties. In Buckinghamshire they varied in individual parishes from 11 shillings per acre at Westbury in the 1760s to 139 shillings per acre at Monks

Risborough in the 1830s. For the county as a whole there was a 140 per cent increase in costs from the 1760s to the turn of the century and a further 94 per cent increase thereafter. This was more exceptional than the general inflation in other prices over the same period [107: *132–3*]. A similar pattern to a greater or lesser degree emerges for the other counties. For Warwickshire the percentage increase was greater, up to 1800 there was a threefold increase and thereafter costs doubled, giving a sixfold increase over the whole period [78: *131*].

Before the 1790s, in Leicestershire, Oxfordshire, Lindsey, Buckinghamshire and Warwickshire, the unit costs per decade were comparable, but thereafter in Buckinghamshire there was ostensibly a disproportionately large increase in enclosure costs. It has been claimed that probably this was due to the more complete manuscript material which is available for Buckinghamshire after 1790. The nature of this material suggests that unit costs before c.1790 were higher than the general source materials have shown. If this turns out to be the case elsewhere it would have the effect of reducing the general rate of increase of enclosure costs before 1790 but increasing the overall unit costs in this earlier period [full argument in 104].

There is another reason why we should be cautious about attaching too much importance to the rate of increase of enclosure costs. Perhaps these costs were small in earlier enclosures because they were simpler enclosures, with fewer owners and other claimants to satisfy, and costs like commissioners' fees which were calculated on a daily rate would have been smaller if enclosures were expeditious. These earlier enclosures were often completed within one or two harvest cycles. Perhaps the more complex, costly enclosures were delayed until market conditions were more favourable, for example during the profit inflation of the Napoleonic wars. The ideal procedure must be to compare information on enclosures with unchanging specifications so that 'the observed increase in costs is a reflection of the increase in benefits, not of an increase in costs for a given enclosure' [74: *142*]. This approach has yet to be tested.

Recent research has established that much common and waste enclosure was financed by selling-off parts of the communal land. In this case there was no direct out-of-pocket expense to the individual landowner, though the cost in the loss of otherwise communal property was great. In Kent, sales of common, all in the nineteenth century, ranged from 6 to 35 per cent of all the land allotted (with a mean of 21 per cent), and in two Middlesex enclosures such sales represented 16 and 28 per cent respectively of all the land allotted [108; *241–2*]. In 20 out of 68 West Sussex enclosures land sales were used to defray public costs. These varied from 1 to 40 per cent of the total land allotted with a mean of 15 per cent [47: *337–41*]. The mean cost of 21 Wiltshire enclosures where land sales took place was 33 shillings per acre, the 8 open field enclosures all fell below this mean whereas the 13 common and waste ones were all above [90: *passim*]. In over 30 North Somerset wasteland enclosures where land sales occurred the range of public costs was from 37 to 199 shillings per acre. These enclosures involved the sale of from 5 to 58 per cent of all the land allotted in individual cases [39: *122–4*]. In this last example, in most cases, the costs did not include a contribution for the tithe owners' fencing, grass seed and general husbandry expenses, and road construction costs, which were all important items in open field enclosures. Thus even in the absence of such weighty items of public costs nevertheless these few examples reveal the vastly more costly nature of common and waste enclosures.

The financial burden of enclosure did not end when the business was formally completed by the commissioners. There were other items of expenditure which were essential if the final improvement of the land was to be maximised, and many of these became a long-term call on the incomes of estates [108: *247*]. This expenditure was not necessarily officially required by the authority vested in the act of enclosure and collected by the commissioners as a public cost, but rather amounted to costs incurred for those fences and buildings which finally completed the improvement. It has been suggested that the final total cost of enclosure, including fencing and other improvement costs, was double the public costs [e.g. 158: *72–81*]. Even this might be an underestimate when we consider that both Martin and Turner have calculated that boundary fences alone often cost as much, when expressed in unit acre terms, as the public costs [78: *140–1, 151*; 157: *303*]. Add to this the cost of subdivision fences and new buildings and it is clear that the full cost of an enclosure was a considerably underestimated burden. Holderness suggests that by 1800 the total cost of an enclosure, including public charges, fencing, ditching and other capital improvements amounted to about £12 per acre, a far cry, even with caution, from the up to £3 otherwise accepted [64: *167*]. He further estimated that the possible capital cost of English parliamentary enclosure was about £10 million in public costs plus a further £19–25 million in capital investment after enclosure [ibid.: *166–7*, the upper bound includes an estimate for underdrainage, the lower bound does not]. These are estimates which did not have the benefit of data from recent local studies of common and waste enclosures. In view of the fact that such enclosures were more costly than their open field counterparts we might consider them as lower bounds.

Without many separate studies of agricultural and enclosure investment such national estimates appear to be meaningless, yet they may have value in comparative terms. The government made loans of £500 million to finance the French wars, so enclosure investment looks inconsiderable by comparison, but the lower bound estimate of £29 million was 50 per cent greater than the £20 million invested in canals between 1750–1815 [P. Mathias, *The First Industrial Nation* (1969), *14*]. In these terms we can wonder whether the diversion of resources into enclosure, let alone agricultural development in general, was large enough to impede the progress of British industrialisation. Probably not, but on the benefit side it may have been enough to release much needed labour for industrial use, enough to raise surplus incomes through productivity gains to service at least part of the capital requirements of industry. In addition, it was probably not enough to prolong the wars with France but enough to ensure that Britain did not starve, and was not bankrupted by otherwise excessive importation of food. Indeed, possibly the enclosure of common and waste after 1800 secured British independence.

(ii) Distribution of public costs

How were the public costs distributed between different items? Taken together the charges for the act, fees to solicitors, commissioners and surveyors, the physical costs such as went into laying new roads and ditches, and the tithe fences are familiar to us [e.g. 97; 78; 89; 157], but there has never been sufficient disaggregation of these items of cost. In contemporary accounts the administrators of enclosure rarely emerge with much credit on the issue of their charges. Homer criticised the solicitors for unnecessarily increasing their bills and fees by attending the petitions at Westminister 'even where there has been no opposition' [13: *107*]. It has also been suggested that enclosure costs were inflated by the practice of commissioners taking on too many commissions at one time [e.g. 106]. One witness to a Select

Committee of 1800 reported that in one enclosure 'the bill of the commissioners came to four guineas, besides their expences. The Act directed only two guineas but they stated they worked double days and therefore were entitled to double fees'. He suggested a prohibition on commissioners taking on more than three enclosures at one time [14: *232*].

This last point is very important. Per enclosure, the commissioners' fees were not a large proportion of total costs, considering the responsibility attached to the job, but their delay and neglect in completing enclosures because they were involved in several at the same time was more injurious to the interested parties than the actual sum of money allowed them [ibid.: *232*]. Whether they made exceptional profits from enclosures, as is sometimes stated, is open to doubt, though quite clearly some of them had very successful careers [106].

Table IV compares the distribution of costs in Warwickshire and Buckinghamshire. In the former county the fees for expenses on travel and entertainment have been separated, whereas for the latter they have been apportioned to the particular administrators who incurred them, usually the commissioners. For 17 Wiltshire enclosures (1743–1847) the comparative distribution of costs was 36 per cent on legal fees (of which 22 per cent was incurred in parliament), 37 per cent on commissioners and surveyors and only 9 per cent for tithe fences and roads [152: *207–8*].

In early Warwickshire enclosures the largest item of cost was the legal expense. It remained high, but so too did all administrative fees. Surely the commissioners were not guilty of the absurd extravagance often attributed to them, especially since the recorded fees were divided among three, five or even seven commissioners who were appointed to each enclosure. The commissioners' profession was certainly a rewarding one but they could not or did not extort exaggerated fees. The solicitors who presented the petitions to Westminster very often became the clerks to the commissions (in Buckinghamshire at least), and the combined legal and clerical fees always came to more than 20 per cent of total costs in Buckinghamshire and more than 30 per cent in Warwickshire, and 36 per cent in Wiltshire. Enclosures provided almost continuous employment for solicitors. They were engaged at every stage: during the pre-act negotiations; petitioning the bill; acting as clerks to the commissioners; and conducting normal land conveyancing for any land

Table IV

Distribution of Enclosure Costs in Warwickshire and Buckinghamshire (in percentages)

Period	Legal fees / Parliamentary fees & solicitors' fees for soliciting the bill	Administration fees / commissioners clerks	Survey	Tithe Owners' fences at public cost	Physical costs (i.e. roads, drains, etc.)	Expenses
Warwickshire						
Pre-1770	36.2	13.1	12.1[a]	5.4	Negligible	11.4
1770–89	40.7[a]	11.1	12.9	18.3	Negligible	2.0
1790–1810	16.8	14.6	10.3	9.3	19.3	2.4
Buckinghamshire						
1770–89	17.9	18.6	13.7	9.7	9.0	18.3
1790–1809	18.2	14.9	14.5	9.2	26.2	11.3
1810–29	13.1	12.7	8.3	8.0	33.5	13.8
Post-1829	18.2	13.5	9.3	5.8	33.6	11.6

[a] In this case the clerks' fees could not easily be separated from the solicitors' fees. It was not unusual for the solicitor to become the clerk. 'Other' costs have been omitted.

Sources: Adapted from J. M. Martin, 'The Cost of Parliamentary Enclosure in Warwickshire', in E. L. Jones (ed.), *Agriculture and Economic Growth in England 1650–1815* (1967), pp. 148–50; M. E. Turner, *Some Social and Economic Considerations of Parliamentary Enclosure in Buckinghamshire, 1738–1865* (Unpublished PhD, University of Sheffield, 1973), pp. 320–4.

exchange, sale, or mortgage which arose because of enclosure [157: *260–5*].

The main features of Table IV are the relatively inexpensive survey, the requirement to fence the tithe allotment at public expense, and the growing importance of the physical costs of making roads, drains and bridges, but particularly roads. Tate suggested that paying for public fencing could put as much as one-seventh on to the bill of all other landowners [97: *265*]. In Warwickshire and Buckinghamshire public fences averaged one-tenth or one-twelfth of total costs. Road costs rarely entered into normal details in accounts until after c.1790, but then they seemed to overwhelm all other charges, representing 25 per cent and more of total costs in Buckinghamshire.

There is a suspicion from recent research that for the earlier period, before 1780, road costs were not included in the cost schedules appended to the enclosure awards. Much post-enclosure expenditure evidently was for completing the road account [157: *ch.8*]. It seemed to be customary in the early enclosures to allot the land before setting out the roads, in which case it is hardly surprising that the road accounts were not included in the general cost schedules, since the roads had not yet been constructed. Even taking into account that road technology in the early period was somewhat primitive, it must be recognised that the roads and other routeways were an authorised part of enclosures, required labour and were nearly always serviced with an acre or more set aside for the collection of stones and gravel. They were substantial structures, upwards of 40 to 60 feet in width in most cases, at least one-third of which was gravelled. With all the evidence it is inconceivable that road costs were as low as the extant accounts for the earlier period suggest. As Curtler stated: 'It is evident that a considerable portion of the expense of enclosures *came after allotment* and was incurred in the making of roads, drains and fences' [18: *166*, partly my emphasis; see also 64: *164*; 11: *90*; 20: *84*]. The roads became the largest single item of expenditure during the period after 1790 when in general we recognise that the unit acre costs of enclosure were high as well. If the cost of roads has been underestimated for the period before 1790 then our entire appreciation of the burden of enclosure costs heretofore has also been underestimated.

5   Investment and Cost:
Part 2, The Social Cost

(i) SOCIAL CONSEQUENCES: THE BACKGROUND TO THE DEBATE

THE evils and excesses of parliamentary enclosure identified by the
Hammonds in the early twentieth century in their denunciation of it
as an agent of mass proletarianisation sustained generations of
students until challenged in the mid-century by scholars who focused
attention more heavily on the earlier origins of both agrarian and
industrial capitalism. It was no longer accepted that parliamentary
enclosure provided the labour force which was channelled to the
factories and it was demonstrated that enclosure was the source of
much sustained new employment in the countryside.

The tone of the debate was perfectly set by the Hammonds who
said that enclosure was a process in which 'the suffrages were not
counted but weighed'. It was landownership strength measured in
property rather than numbers which influenced parliament, through
the custom that to pass an act for enclosure it was usually necessary to
gain the consent of those who owned two-thirds or more of the acres
proposed for enclosure, rather than the consent of two-thirds or more
of the total number of landowners [22: *25* in 4th edition]. The modern
form of this is Thompson's observation that: 'Enclosure (when all the
sophistications are allowed for) was a plain enough case of class
robbery, played according to fair rules of property and law laid down
by a parliament of property-owners and lawyers' [102: *237–8*]. To
have recourse to parliament also indicated that local dissent was
present. More important, the nature of parliament in responding to a
property measure rather than a head count indicated that the dissent
was by the many against the few, the small against the big, the
defenceless against the powerful authority which elected parliament
in the first place.

The examples the Hammonds used to demonstrate their case were,
however, clearly biased and a simple empiric refutation by weight of

alternative examples would have been easy. But such a refutation did not immediately come, and so the enclosures of Otmoor in Oxfordshire, Haut Huntre in Lincolnshire, King's Sedgemoor in Somerset, and others, passed into legend as the exemplars of enclosure with associated social evils. That they were enclosures mainly of large commons, on which, relatively speaking, vast populations depended for essential services like fuel-gathering, was almost lost in the polemics of the case. Quite clearly the landless and those with tenuously held or tenuously established common rights suffered the loss of those commons greatly. But they were not typical commons enclosures, let alone typical enclosures in general. The Hammonds concentrated on the small farmer, the cottager, and the squatter, and, not surprisingly, concluded that they above all others were severely damaged by enclosure.

Apart from an empirical study by Davies (1927), a challenge to the Hammonds did not emerge until the 1940s, when Tate largely refuted the bad press which parliamentary enclosure had received, touching upon such issues as opposition, the relationship between the enclosers and members of parliament, and dispelling any notions of collusion or conspiracy [93–6; and see also 79]. The Hammonds, however, remained the popular interpretation, reinforced as they were through the researches in the 1930s of the Soviet historian Lavrovsky [24–5; 70]. He established how important the church was in collaborating to bring about enclosures with the vast transfer of land from lay to church hands through tithe commutation. This was the annulment of church tithes, previously paid in money or in kind, by substituting a quantity of land. The net result was that the church became one of the great landowning institutions in many English villages though entirely at the expense in land and costs to the mass of proprietors [24: 71]. This land transfer has been well illustrated for Leicestershire, among other counties [67: *499–500*]. An important aspect which is often neglected, however, is that in many areas lay tithes were more important than clerical ones, and this brought about a land transfer from some lay hands to other lay hands. In Warwickshire over 17 per cent of common field and common was transferred in this way, of which about one-half went to lay impropriators, and in Buckinghamshire the tithe owners received up to 20 per cent of the land allotted at enclosure [77: *37*; 157: *78*]. Tithe commutation was calculated at about one-fifth or one-sixth of the open field land and one-eighth or ninth of the commons in the south Midlands. This level of tithe

65

commutation was almost certainly in excess of the value of the original tithe, and so we might observe that the transfer of commuted lands was effectively a redistribution of income. At the same time it was a once and for all commutation, the easing of the annual burden of tithes was much welcomed by landowners, and it left many clerics with unaccustomed landlords' responsibilities.

In eleven Suffolk parishes enclosed between 1797–1814 Lavrovsky found that there was a numerical predominance of small landowners (owning less than 25 acres), and the emergence of a small group of middle and well-to-do owners (owning up to 150 acres), and richer ones (owning over 150 acres) who were approaching capitalist sizes [25]. In another study he found that for a parish enclosed in 1803 landowners who were not defined as members of the nobility, gentry or church held nearly 40 per cent of the land but that the earlier the enclosure the weaker was their position. Thus in a parish enclosed in 1797 they held nearly 24 per cent but in a parish enclosed in 1780 they held less than 6 per cent [70]. The implication was that for early enclosed parishes the peasantry (as he referred to them) were almost extinct but in later ones they were stronger, and this may have been a reason for delayed enclosure, the recalcitrance of a strong peasant society which was persuaded by the profit inflation of the French wars to enclose. Evidence from Buckinghamshire supports this approach [157: *chs 4, 5*].

Such studies concentrated attention on the dynamic nature of the social and economic countryside, in which enclosure played a part, but not necessarily a dominant part, in landownership adjustments. It followed that the real issue was not necessarily the social upheaval at enclosure but more broadly the social upheaval caused by all elements of agrarian capitalism. Recent understanding of eighteenth-century rural society in England suggests that the fracture of landownership among a large number of small proprietors was a reason for delayed enclosure. In Kesteven resident lords and monastic foundations coincided with early enclosure (i.e. before the eighteenth century) while the stronger the freeholder tradition the later the enclosure [82]. In Warwickshire there was considerable social differentiation according to chronology of enclosure, not unrelated to the difference between 'open' and 'close' parishes [77: *22–7*]. The earliest enclosures in this county (before 1750) were promoted by the squirearchy seeking to consolidate estates, but after 1750 the inspiration came from freeholders trying to improve farming in general. After 1780 the growing food market and sharply rising land values brought about the enclosure of the great overcrowded 'open' parishes, in which, though landownership remained widely dispersed among small owners, big landlords were still a substantial force. And it was in these parishes enclosed after 1780 that the most striking post-enclosure changes took place [for Leicestershire see 67].

Small or medium-sized landowners, as well as large ones, could have held enclosure in abeyance, albeit against a resentful squire-archy, church and parliament, only to relent and give their sanction to enclose when conditions of the moment suited them. This might have occurred during the inflation of the Napoleonic wars [77: *29*; 107: *ch.7*]. Some of these 'peasants', in fact, were behaving like capitalists, and we must recognise that a strong, commercially minded small landownership structure is not incompatible with a Marxist interpre-tation of the eighteenth century. Yet Lavrovsky also argued that through enclosure the peasantry as a whole was weakened, for example by the expropriation of lands through tithe commutation, and in general that there was a concentration of wealth and influence towards the larger and wealthier landowners and the poorer and smaller ones were either weakened or disappeared altogether. These and other general observations of the social effects of enclosure were not to go unchallenged.

(ii) J. D. CHAMBERS AND REVISION

Leading the revisionists in the period after the Second World War was J. D. Chambers, himself a product of the East Midlands peasantry, and it was from his own neighbourhood that he gathered his evidence [43–5]. In Lindsey, Derbyshire and Nottinghamshire he largely confirmed Davies's earlier (but partly overlooked) findings that from c.1790–1830 there was an increase in the number of owner-occupiers in general. At its most basic the owner-occupier was the symbol of independence, he was the peasant. Subsequently Grigg confirmed these broad trends for south Lincolnshire for the period 1798–1832, but in Wiltshire, one of the first non-Midlands-type open field areas to be studied in depth, there was no significant change in owner-occupancy related to enclosure [61: *87–8*; 60; 152: *ch.7*].

Whether the language used was in terms of peasants, owner-occupiers or independent men, the scene was set for the next major area of debate. Chambers could, if he wished, have suggested that far from a decline in the position of the independent 'peasant', his standing in the community was strengthened. But was it a period during which the large peasants grew at the expense of the small, or was there a general resurgence of small peasant farming? Davies had found that the growth was actually greatest in the group of the smallest owners, those possessing fewer than 20 acres, and the chief decline was in a group of middle-sized owners:

> we are therefore dealing with owners of from 20–100 acres, whose farms were too large to work with family labour alone and too small to permit the accumulation of a reserve against adversity; they were big enough to be dependent on the grain market and to be vitally affected by its fluctuations. [43: *122*]

The smaller owners were better able to cope with the post-Napoleonic wars agricultural depression because their farms were supplementary rather than basic to their subsistence. However, Davies's estimates of acreage size groups were based on calculations which converted the money evidence in the land tax into an acreage equivalent. Chambers questioned this procedure, as did Grigg, Mingay and Martin subsequently [60; 84; 76; 80; see also 105 and the latest land tax debate in *Econ.Hist.Rev.*, 35 (3), Aug.1982]. The most that might be conceded to Davies is that those paying the smallest sums, less than £1 (which at 1 shilling per acre gives up to 20 acres), increased in numbers up to 1830 (though not necessarily continuously nor uniformly over time) and those paying £1–5 declined in numbers.

Chambers next turned specifically to the role of enclosure in producing landownership structural changes. In those parishes where enclosure took place at the time the land tax was available (1780–1832) he found that there were larger numbers of owner-occupiers than in parishes which were already enclosed [43: *123*]. The more ancient the enclosure the weaker was freeholder society and the stronger was the absentee squirearchy in the late eighteenth century. Conversely, those places which in the late eighteenth century were awaiting enclosure had a more broadly based resident freeholder society, a peasant society.

Chambers partly upset his own arguments when he pointed out that much of the increase in the land tax paid by the smallest contributors resulted from the recognition at enclosure of the legal rights of some cottagers and squatters who otherwise were landless. In many respects he was responding to the Edwardian criticism of enclosure as a social evil, as the creator of a labour surplus, and his 1947 study was particularly aimed at Herman Levy's contention that 'the small plots of the cottagers and little farmers, holdings of from one to eight acres or so, on which the occupiers had mostly raised livestock and dairy produce, practically vanished altogether in the course of the Napoleonic Wars' [44: *16*, quoting from H. Levy, *Large and Small Holdings: a Study in English Agricultural Economics* (1911), p. 17]. Chambers contended that the marginal unit of production (i.e. 25–100 acres) was the most vulnerable, was the likely victim of enclosure. This included tenants of comparable size who may have felt the post-enclosure rent increases more severely than both the smaller units where holdings were supplementary rather than basic to needs, and the larger units which had developed accumulated reserves of capital [43: *126*]. What was not pointed out was the economic ramifications of the Napoleonic wars and the subsequent post-war depression. Perhaps owners and tenants of these 'marginal' units had most to gain from the inflation in agricultural prices and incomes during the war, but they also had most to lose in the subsequent downturn. These 'marginal' owners may have promoted enclosures during the war years, they may have held it in abeyance before 1790, but they certainly burnt their fingers in the aftermath of war having overcommitted resources on enclosure at fixed high interest rates when the bulk of their repayments occurred in the post-war deflation.

Hunt's point is worth considering at this stage. In Leicestershire between 1790–1830 there was a decline in the number of small owners, but this decline was observable in parishes quite unconnected with recent or current enclosure as well as in those recently affected by enclosure. This suggests important consequences arising from the profit inflation of the Napoleonic wars followed by deflation in the subsequent depression [67: *503–4*]. Great sums of capital were expended by people during the profitable times of the war, not only on enclosure, and much of the time they borrowed when real interest rates were low (a point made in Chapter 3 above). They found that during the depression their repayments remained unchanged but their incomes were squeezed. A second point is that if small owners were in decline, whether persistently or simply ultimately, the larger owners, over 100–150 acres, were growing in landownership strength. They were engrossing but this was a feature not necessarily confined to parishes of parliamentary enclosure, though perhaps it was more evident in those parishes. Perhaps this was a case of selling out by small absentee owners while land was rising in value, as much as selling by residents because of the cost of enclosure [ibid.: *504–5*]. In Warwickshire though, there was a trend detectable before 1780 which continued to 1825, for the proportion of land held by owners of from 4–100 acres to decline in parishes where enclosure had taken place or was taking place, and it was strongest in those parishes enclosed after 1780 [77: *35*]. The debate had turned full circle, back to a consideration of the small owners [80].

The argument that parliamentary enclosure was a source of English industrial proletarianisation, that it had created a landless agricultural class which marched to the cotton mills, was once again open to discussion. Chambers had conceded that a certain amount of buying out of freeholds and leases for lives was a prelude to enclosure. But, even if those dispossessed owners became tenants, it may have been within a system of larger tenancies. Some of them remained landless or replaced existing tenants. The process is unclear but a rationalisation of tenancies effectively reduced the number of tenant occupiers. The suspicion is that there was a filter which produced some degree of landlessness over and above that which prevailed anyway. The discovery that there was a good deal of differentiation within and between parish landownership structures is not evidence of when or how such differentiation took place. As Hunt found for Leicestershire:

> It would be wrong to say . . . that the engrossing of land by a few large proprietors and the almost complete disappearance of the small landowner generally preceded and facilitated parliamentary enclosure by removing a class who would otherwise have opposed it,

and in Buckinghamshire it is difficult to establish a special land market as a prelude to enclosure [67: *501*; 157: *104–11*]. Much the same can be said for Warwickshire, though there are isolated examples which tend towards a theory of estate engrossment before enclosure [77: *34, 36*]. The beneficiaries of this adjustment in landownership profiles were the large landowners and also large tenant farmers. In particular the proportion of land owned by freeholders in possession of 100–199 acres increased [ibid.: *36–7*], the middle-to-richer peasants of Lavrovsky's model.

However, Chambers' findings did not immediately come under detailed attack. That parliamentary enclosure had little effect on small landholders became, for a time, the new conventional wisdom, reinforced by his joint work with G. E. Mingay and restated in Mingay's pamphlet about small farmers [46: *ch.4*; 85; see also 59; 83]. The first reaction was a mild yet clear enough counter-revisionism, pointing out the importance of viewing the history of landownership over a longer time period. As Saville put it 'Nowhere save in Britain was the peasantry virtually eliminated *before* the acceleration of economic growth that is associated with the development of industrial capitalism, and of the many special features of early industrialisation in Britain none is more striking than the presence of a rapidly growing proletariat in the countryside' [91: *250*].

Authors of all political shades have couched their arguments in terms of the 'peasantry'. It is a term which seems to have as many definitions as historians trying to unscramble its origins and demise. Saville tried to clear some of the ground by drawing a sharper distinction between the peasant as a tenant farmer and as an owner farmer. He objected to the confusing use of small farmer, small occupier, and family farmer when the revisionists were really referring to the small tenant farmer: 'what is not acceptable is that this emphasis upon the small *tenant* farmer should be used to blur a fact of change which is more significant, namely the elimination from the English rural economy of an independent peasant class' [ibid.: *253*]. The preoccupation of historians with technical changes in the history of the agricultural revolution ignores more significant long-term structural changes and the decline of an independent, owner-occupying, peasant class. When they did begin to decline or even disappear is a more important question than dating their final decline, because if this process presaged a subsequent development in society then the genesis was crucial. Though the small farm by the end of the eighteenth century and even up to the mid-nineteenth century remained an important feature in rural areas, especially in Wales and Scotland and in west and north-west England, its survival obscured the other important feature of British farming, the emergence of 'the large farm using hired labour and working wholly for the market', that is the emergence of capitalist farming and the existence of a substantial rural proletariat, a feature quite without comparison in most of Continental Europe [ibid.: *258*]. There can be some confusion, however, when such disparate regions are summarised in this way. For example, in Scotland, Saville fails to point out that the small farm was always a tenant farm. Does this mean that in the absence of owner-occupancy there was no Scottish peasantry? Of course not, but it does mean that we must be more sensitive to regional and cultural variations. Nevertheless, Saville's attempt to unscramble the peasant owner and occupier from the wider discussion of farmers, which included tenants, was necessary. In so doing he certainly misjudged the regional differences but more important, he may have underplayed this other important feature of the British rural scene, namely tenant farming [in this context see 56; 83; 85].

Working from Gregory King's base of 1688 and recognising the imperfections in King's estimates Mingay has placed the good or bad fortunes of the tenant farmer into a subsequent chronology of change. In 1688 the 180,000 freeholders exceeded the number of tenants estimated at 150,000. These figures include large as well as small tenants. Mingay suggests that two-thirds of all farmers were small, that is in ownership or occupation of 20–100 acres (mainly within Lavrovsky's middle-peasant-size group), in which case there were 220,000 of them (presumably in the same ratio of freeholders to tenants, or 100,000 tenants of this group). Late nineteenth-century evidence suggests a decline of one-third of farmers, whether owners or tenants, since King's day. Small farmers probably numbered 130–140,000, giving a decline from a conjectural 220,000 small farmers in King's day of 40 per cent. But this ignores the more important feature that small farmers were still numerous at the end of the nineteenth century and outnumbered farmers of more than 100 acres [85: *14*]. Furthermore, Mingay claims that when the tenants are separated from the owner-occupiers the decline in the former was limited, while the decline of the latter was more dramatic [ibid.: *14*]. Though the trend of the two centuries before the late nineteenth favoured large units there is no evidence to show that the decline of small farms was either rapid or general [ibid.: *15–16*]. Finally, the probable timing of the major decline was put not during the period of parliamentary enclosure but rather in the seventeenth and early eighteenth centuries [ibid.: *26–32*]; which certainly takes the focus away from parliamentary enclosure but places it firmly in the narrower period of change before the mid-eighteenth century, a period perhaps not of such gradual change as supposed but rather of dramatic pruning of the small owner-occupier and some decline of the tenants.

There is some supporting evidence from eighteenth-century Scotland where, regardless of enclosure, there was a 'general movement in every part of Lowland Scotland to lay down larger farms and nearly always larger farms meant fewer tenants; dispossession and eviction became a common experience', and such changes 'had become a common folk memory in the 1790s [131: *135*]. In this case it was the eviction of tenants that occurred rather than the elimination, by whatever means, of owners and owner-occupiers as in England. In Scotland the term peasant refers to a tenant farming on a small scale or primarily for subsistence, as we have already indicated. In Roxburghshire and Berwickshire, which with the Lothians were pioneer agrarian areas, there were considerable reductions in tenant numbers in the eighteenth century. This resulted from the removal of runrig, and although there is ample evidence of enclosure and adjustments in farm layout, it was not necessarily or indeed primarily connected with the rationalisation of the tenantry and removal of runrig [126: *121–7*]. In Aberdeenshire in the late seventeenth century the differentiation of rural society was extreme and the stratification of the peasantry, regardless of enclosure, was almost complete when compared with England [125: *14–19*]. Here, enclosures were not linked with social evils, save some early eighteenth-century activity against the fencing of land, the loss of common pasturage, and the eviction of tenants associated with an increase in the cattle trade with England after the Union [130; 144: *116*]. Enclosure aided and abetted the process of structural change but itself was not the only nor necessarily the dominant factor in the move to capitalist agriculture which, after a hesitant start, flourished after 1780 in Scotland. In particular rich 'peasants' became 'capitalist farmers' during the profit inflation of the Napoleonic wars. Even later, however, there remained in areas like Aberdeenshire very large numbers of small tenants cultivating the edge of the moor and supplying labour to the larger ones [125: *20–1*].

(iv) THE RECENT DEBATES

Further research built upon Chambers' findings and questioned them. The outcome was a revolution in thinking concerning the economic costs and social consequences of enclosure. The debates are still alive and can be readily summarised [based mainly on 77; 78; 80; 104; 105; 107; 108; 111; 155]. The cost of enclosure was far in excess of what was ever imagined. This was partly because little regard had been given in the literature to fencing costs and other costs of improvement over and above what were often relatively small size costs of administration. Costs could not be deferred over any considerable time, certainly rarely as long as a full harvest cycle. Payment of costs was made in a number of ways and though if land was sold off it eased the social consequences, this practice was relatively narrowly confined to common and waste enclosures and nineteenth-century enclosures [39; 47; 108: *240–2*]. Where it did apply to the enclosure of open fields it reduced the size of individual allotments, which in some cases, with other reductions for tithe commutation and the appeasement of manorial rights, were reduced to uneconomic units. As a result many landowners, especially small ones, sold off their estates. On top of these problems and aggravations, unit costs were disproportionately larger for small estates [78; 152: *202–6*].

High costs could mean an inability to raise finances sufficient to meet them. The sale of land was sometimes necessary, sometimes inevitable, further reducing small-owner proprietorship. Improved incomes through improved productivity were insufficient in one year to cover expenses, and the raising of mortgages, though permitted, was set at a level which did not reasonably cover the full cost of an enclosure [108: *242–5*]. Mortgages therefore were often not taken up; similarly the diversion of income from one estate to pay for enclosing another was the privilege of a limited number of wealthier interested parties [ibid.: *245–7*].

It can be suggested (from evidence from the clayland counties of the Midlands) that these last points resulted in the hasty sale of many estates either upon or shortly after enclosure. This 'turnover' of land and landowners was particularly evident with small landowners and small estates [105; 80; 155: *208–33, 412–31*]. Chambers had discovered that far from small landowners disappearing because of enclosure, their numbers actually increased during the Napoleonic wars when enclosure was at its most intense. A head count from the land tax showed an increase in the proportion of owner-occupiers during the course of the war. The owner-occupiers in question epitomised peasant ownership in the guise of (relatively) self-sufficient man. But the head count, while a valuable exercise in the argument against the disappearance of the peasantry, disguised a much more important feature of the countryside. The heads in question changed faces in large numbers and with remarkable coincidence with enclosure. The rate of turnover within two or three years of enclosure in Buckinghamshire was over 30 per cent of the original owners, with 40 and 50 per cent as the norm and 60 per cent as not unusual [105: *568*]. In Warwickshire not only was this turnover coincident with enclosure, but also there was an absolute decline in the number of heads in the rural social structure in certain landowning groups, in particular of small landowners who declined 'as a class by perhaps 25 per cent within a decade of enclosure' [80: *343*]. The same absolute decline did not generally occur in Buckinghamshire. The only way the head count grew was in the sense identified by Chambers, through the recognition at enclosure of what was one form or other of common right. A failure to appreciate this point fully surely distorted Chambers' overall appraisal of enclosure.

If the changes took place, who were the new personnel? At the moment, on insecure or limited data, we might suggest that in many cases there was an influx of people quite unconnected with the parishes in question, merchants and other townspeople wishing to gain a social foothold in the countryside, widows and spinsters investing idle funds, and a move towards absentee landlordism in general, as well as local manoeuvring on the lower rungs of the agricultural and social ladder. The composite 'turnover' of farmers (in this case meant to mean owner-occupiers as well as tenants) is yet in an early state of investigation, but Walton offers the following tentative conclusions from his Oxfordshire study. Enclosure was accompanied by an increase in the rate at which holdings of both owner-occupiers and tenant farmers changed hands; this also provided the opportunity for completely new occupiers and tenants to enter the county as well as a redistribution of existing ones. However, the social consequences of this residential mobility did not necessarily result in the dispossession of small owner-occupiers or the extinction of small tenancies [111: esp. *251*]. Perhaps this identifies the opportunity to renegotiate leases afforded by the provisions of the acts of enclosure.

The observation of all these changes taking place must surely have aroused suspicion and hostility in places yet to be enclosed. There is growing interest in the opposition to enclosure, not only opposition to the enclosure of commons like Otmoor so popularised by the

Hammonds and others, but also opposition to open field enclosures by sitting tenants, owners, and those who possessed only common rights. While the nature of opposition is still little understood, it is evident below the surface both in the parliamentary record and in local history [95; 155; 79; esp. *107–8*; 157: *ch.6*].

Whether or not these fresh approaches give comfort to Marxist interpretations is questionable, since revised Marxist views now suggest that parliamentary enclosure was a mopping-up process, the final straw in a long-drawn-out saga of peasant appropriation by the march of capitalism (note the change of nomenclature, however, appropriation meaning buying out rather than expropriation, which means dispossession by force or conspiracy) [103: *ch.2*]. The evidence now seems to show both a history of peasant survival, to a greater or less degree, well into the nineteenth century, and peasants appropriating peasants as much as peasants being appropriated by the social and economic classes from above. Perhaps the time is ripe to review Rae's long-lost suggestion that the crisis for the peasantry (he used the term yeomanry) came in the post-Napoleonic wars crisis of depressed agricultural incomes [26; see also 36]. Perhaps the decades of enclosure can be viewed as ones in which capitalism emerged and built upon earlier movements towards commercial farming but was not confined to or synonymous with the misleading metaphor of 'bigness'. The peasant survival into the ninetenth century and the peasant turnover studies itemised earlier therefore might be regarded as commercialisation by small owner-occupiers, even of those who did not employ non-family labour, and therefore the disappearance of subsistence farming. Though commercialisation was not constrained by small size, yet it was also not a once and for all process everywhere at the same time. Thus we get the protracted survival of the peasantry which recent enclosure studies have identified.

(v) ENCLOSURE AND LABOUR SUPPLY

Was enclosure a crucial agent (not necessarily the only one) in the recruitment of an industrial labour force by which the expropriation of small owners and tenants swelled the ranks of the rural labourers, creating a surplus labour force in the countryside which, coupled with the more efficient use of labour in enclosed farms, marched to the towns seeking industrial work? Chambers addressed this important Marxist model of proletarianisation. In particular he attacked the idea that the enclosure commissioners were a capitalist pressgang. Maurice Dobb had suggested that any alternative implied that the emergence of a reserve army of labour arose from a growing population creating more hands than could be fed from the labour of the soil: 'If this were the true story, one might have reason to speak of a proletariat as a natural rather than an institutional creation and to treat accumulation of capital and the growth of a proletariat as autonomous and independent processes. But this idyllic picture fails to accord with the facts' [quoted in 45: *94*]. Chambers did not question the notion of an institutional origin of the proletariat but whether enclosure was the relevant institution. The growth of the proletariat was not separate from capital accumulation but the nature of their relationship was obscure [ibid.: *95*].

Chambers saw no general association between enclosure and population movements; he found that it was just as likely that the size of the population rose after enclosure without migrating, and that the population growth in mining, industrial and textile villages in Nottinghamshire was not significantly greater than growth in agricultural communities in the first three decades of the nineteenth century [ibid.: *101*]. His argument rested on demographic change rather than institutional change (or at least not on enclosure or the power of a landed ruling class as the institution). 'The only answer can be that at some unspecified time in the eighteenth century the movement of population had taken an upward turn in village and town alike and provided an entirely new supply of human material beside which the dislocations caused by enclosure were of a secondary importance' [ibid.: *120–2*]. So it was the unabsorbed surplus of rural population and not the main body which became the industrial workforce, and this surplus was the consequence of demographic change and not of institutional change, that is to say, not of enclosure [see also 30].

Chambers' exclusive use of Nottinghamshire as a study area has been criticised by Crafts as likely to produce a biased result. A larger study of the south and east Midlands in general found no evidence for an increase in population after enclosure, and therefore no evidence to advance Chambers' thesis of greater labour-using activity after enclosure. Moreover, there was a positive correlation between enclosure and out-migration [52: *176–7, 180–1*].

Crafts has further suggested that though the income elasticity of demand for food in the eighteenth century was high, a declining *share* of labour in agriculture was able to meet the extra food requirements of a growing population. Absolute numbers in agriculture actually rose, but proportionately slower than the growth of population in general. Output per man therefore rose substantially and the 'new farming' (not just enclosure) allowed the agricultural sector to raise this unit output per annum by the fuller employment of workers previously underemployed for much of the year. He concludes that though general labour opportunities rose, the increase in labour productivity and the declining share of the population engaged in agriculture in the face of a demographic revolution is the same as saying that in relative terms there was a release of labour [53: esp. *167*].

If enclosure did increase labour opportunities, for example for the construction and upkeep of fences, drains and roads, which was important to Chambers' argument, it opens up the intriguing prospect that enclosure, while it was efficient for agriculture, was inefficient in other ways; it absorbed and held back labour which otherwise may have become available for industry. Therefore for optimal resource allocation enclosure may have retained labour in agriculture which would have been better employed in industry [33: *408*]. We need to address the question of labour use and whether the general spirit of the agricultural revolution was labour-intensive or not.

In Lowland Scotland the tendency was towards the employment of fewer hands, and enclosure was not necessarily responsible for this. Even if the new husbandry improved unit labour productivity there was often a trade-off because of an extension of acreage under crops, at least until 1830 [131: *145–9*]. Even where the appearance and consolidation of larger than average farm units occurred by a process of joint tenancy, which inevitably led to the displacement of some tenants, there was not necessarily a flight from the land. In Aberdeenshire this process led to crofting on the improved fringes of the newly enclosed farms thus bringing much new land into cultivation [123: *74*]; and in some, not all, Highland areas agrarian changes created new settlements after 1750 and advanced cultivation into marginal lands. It was the post-Napoleonic wars collapse of prices which brought about displacement, eviction and clearance, and it continued up to and beyond the mid-nineteenth century [ibid.: *74*]. Besides, rural-urban or overseas migration just as easily demonstrates the pull effect from industry and the New World as it does the push effect from agriculture. In the Lothians there is evidence of this pull effect from industry, but equally, where a new labour-intensive activity like turnip cultivation was introduced it served to anchor labour to the village [142: esp. *xxviii–xxix*]. In yet other areas there was the breakdown of a dual economy, for example with the decline of handloom weaving in the mid-nineteenth century, which in turn led to the displacement of rural labour [131: *153, 156*].

Of vital importance is the issue of relative factor prices, in our case the relative movements of rent and wages. If land prices were rising relative to wages (as was the case from the limited empirical evidence) then increases in labour usage at enclosure may reflect a substitution effect of labour for land, offsetting what would have been a lower labour-land ratio caused by labour-saving techniques [33: *415*]. In other words, enclosure accommodated an increase in labour opportunities not out of labour intensity but because of movements in the relative prices of factors of production; the increased returns to land and the relatively decreased returns to labour. If this kept labour on the land it should also be seen in relation to the price of other labour uses, such as in industry. Wages in industry were higher than wages in agriculture. This could lead to an ultimate turnabout in the Marxist view of this history; enclosure anchoring the labour force on the land and industry trying to prise it off. Therefore if relative rural depopulation occurred, the institutional creation of a labour force was not enclosure nor agrarian capitalism, but industry itself. This is an important theoretical twist, and allows speculation on the role of enclosure in raising agricultural productivity so that a decreasing share of the labour force could provide a greater quantity of agricultural produce for an increasing non-agricultural labour force.

Finally, it has been argued that enclosure allocated resources more efficiently, the benefits of innovation exceeding the costs of introducing them, both the transactions costs and those costs required to differentiate property rights and create exclusive as distinct from communal ownership [for example, there may be costs involved in buying out opposition to enclosure, for which see 74: *134–8*; see also 32; 54]. The benefits can be measured as per capita productivity gains which ultimately shifted a growing proportion of the labour force to non-agricultural employment [33: *418*]. This is the same as saying that enclosure created, through efficiency gains, a surplus of labour which was eventually funnelled to industry, and not, as Chambers and the most recent traditional view said, of increasing labour opportunities. It seems to me that the way forward now is to investigate this approach more fully and to point out that the enclosure of common and waste should have produced the largest increases in unit labour productivity and therefore the largest reductions in labour. Common rights were the most intangible, non-exclusive property rights available. They were, therefore, the least productive aspect of village life and therefore offered the greatest possible benefits from enclosure, even at the high costs of achieving exclusive ownership. The enclosure of commons and wastes therefore should have produced a great shake out of unproductive commonality enjoyed by landless labourers, squatters, commoners and even small owners, who would collectively emerge as the reserve army of labour destined for the factories and towns. If this was the case, and it has yet to be tested, then the argument which maintains that enclosure induced productivity gains is strengthened, but the debate over the social distress caused by enclosure turns full circle, because it was these same socio-economic groups who were, according to the Hammonds' tradition, the gravest casualties of enclosure.

6 Conclusions

THERE were significant variations in the pattern of parliamentary enclosure across space and through time. There were equally significant variations in the land types which were enclosed. Two major peaks of activity can be identified, one before 1780 and the other during the period of the French Revolutionary and Napoleonic wars. These two peaks must be considered as separate events, separate in time of course, but also distinguishable in terms of location and the underlying economic motivation for them. Early (i.e. pre-1750) enclosures on the clay soils, especially the heavy clays of the Midlands, took place often with an eye to changing land use from traditional open arable fields into pastures, to take advantage of the comparative advantage these soils had for growing grass in preference to crops during a time of improved living standards, when dietary demand switched partially to a reduced bread and increased meat and dairy products consumption. These early enclosures issued into a major period of enclosing which peaked in the late 1760s and 1770s. The second peak of activity, after 1790 and reaching its height in the first decade of the nineteenth century, brought about the improvement of lighter soils, this time, on the whole, for maintaining and improving arable output, and also brought into cultivation much marginal land, the commons and wastes of the uplands, fenlands, heaths and moors, as well as residual wastes in lowland areas.

A number of economic factors can be identified which we may, by intuition and observation, suppose determined the timing and extent of the two enclosure movements of our period. These factors included inputs like changing prices, availability of money, changing population and other market forces; and outputs in terms of additions to incomes, such as improved rents, and efficiency gains through improved yields and larger output which raised incomes for farmers and landlords alike. The identification of these economic factors also helps to explain why the open fields and unproductive wastes persisted as long as they did. The retarding influence of the open fields on the improvement of British agriculture is subject to some debate, but then so also is the supposed and measured efficiency gain of enclosed fields over open ones. In general the open fields could be adjusted to a certain extent to meet changing economic circumstances but they were not completely adjustable. But overall there was an efficiency gain to be derived from farming in severalty. In the past we may have overestimated the aggregate additions to income, so we certainly must consider the possibility of a redistribution of income away from the small owners and farmers, whose inefficiency was measured by their lack of capital to finance agricultural improvement, to the larger landowners. This leads rather conveniently to a summary of the social consequences of parliamentary enclosure.

The social consequences are now subject to significant revisions. This is based on the economic cost of enclosures and the ability, or lack of ability, of landowners to finance them. In general the cost of enclosure was higher than previously thought. Early assessments failed to take into full account the costs of fencing and other physical costs of improvement over and above the sometimes small-scale costs of administration. A realisation that costs were larger than previously assessed has inspired a fresh approach to the possible social repercussions of enclosure. In general, and admittedly based mainly on evidence from the arable heartland of the Midland counties, it looks as though there was a considerable turnover in landowning personnel. Even if there was not a decrease in the numbers of landowners, and in particular in the numbers of the smaller owner-occupiers, the epitome of the independent peasant class, nevertheless many of these owners sold up at or shortly after enclosure. They were replaced by what appear to be people from their own agricultural and social class, though there is considerable scope for solid research on this issue. In addition, evidence showing that the number of owner-occupiers actually increased in some areas at certain times should not disguise this other consequence of enclosure, the faces and names attached to those numbers often did change dramatically. Besides, the recorded increase in owner-occupiers may be an illusion because owners of common rights only were recorded for the first time as landowners when their rights were transformed from a customary property right into a physical one. Often, these cottagers and other common right owners were the first to sell up their allotments. These newly acquired lands were often very small in size, incapable of supplementing their incomes in the way the commons and wastes had done, for example by providing pasturage for their few animals. They were also disproportionately more costly to enclose and fence than larger allotments. Small owners also had difficulty in meeting enclosure expenses and often sold up at enclosure. In addition there is evidence of a rationalisation of tenancies, though this aspect is still little understood and underresearched.

Thus, if there was an increasing turnover in the land market, and if there was a rationalisation of ownership and tenancy at the poorer end of the scale, including small owners and tenant farmers, cottagers, squatters and the landless, it brings into fresh focus the appearance of a landless labour force to fuel the fire of industrialisation, especially if enclosure improved labour productivity rather than extended labour opportunities. This is certainly the message from the most recent researches. Notwithstanding the demographic revolution which was in train and creating more hands than could be gainfully employed in an improved agricultural industry, enclosure is again under scrutiny as a possible contributor to the industrial labour force.

Bibliography

ABBREVIATIONS

AHR	*Agricultural History Review*
EcHR	*Economic History Review*, second series unless stated otherwise
EEH	*Explorations in Economic History*
JEEH	*Journal of European Economic History*
SGM	*Scottish Geographical Magazine*
TrIBG	*Transactions and Papers of the Institute of British Geographers*

(a) REVIEW AND BIBLIOGRAPHY

[1] J. Blum, 'Review Article. English Parliamentary Enclosure', *Journal of Modern History*, 103 (1981).
[2] J. G. Brewer, *Enclosures and the Open Fields: A Bibliography* (1972).
[3] R. Morgan, *Dissertations on British Agrarian History* (1981).
[4] M. E. Turner, 'Recent Progress in the Study of Parliamentary Enclosure', *The Local Historian*, 12 (Feb. 1976).

(b) SOURCES

[5] I. H. Adams, *Directory of Former Scottish Commonties* (Scottish Record Society, 2, 1971).
[6] I. Bowen, *The Great Inclosures of Common Lands in Wales* (1914).
[7] T. I. J. Jones, *Acts of Parliament Concerning Wales 1714–1901* (1959).
[8] Return, 'Return of Commons (Inclosure Awards)', *Parliamentary Papers – House of Commons*, 50 (1904).
[9] Return, 'Return of Inclosure Acts', *Parliamentary Papers – House of Commons*, 399 (1914).
[10] W. E. Tate, *A Domesday of English Enclosure Acts and Awards* (1978).

(c) CONTEMPORARY

[11] Board of Agriculture, *General Report on Enclosures* (1808).
[12] T. Davis, *General View of the Agriculture of Wiltshire* (1811).
[13] H. Homer, *An Essay on the Nature and Method of Ascertaining the Specific Shares of Proprietors upon the Inclosure of Common Fields* (1766).
[14] Reports, 'Three Reports from the Select Committee Appointed to take into Consideration the Means of Promoting the Cultivation and Improvement of the Waste, Uninclosed and Unproductive Lands in the Kingdom', *Parliamentary Papers, House of Commons Select Committee Reports*, 9 (1795–1801).
[15] T. Stone, *Suggestions for Rendering the Inclosure of Common Fields and Waste Lands a Source of Population and Riches* (1787).
[16] A. Young, *The Farmer's Tour through the East of England* (1771).
[17] ——, *General View of the Agriculture of Oxfordshire* (1813).

(d) BOOKS AND ARTICLES PRE-1940 (ENGLAND AND WALES)

[18] W. H. R. Curtler, *The Enclosure and Redistribution of our Land* (1920).
[19] E. Davies, 'The Small Landowner 1780–1832, in the Light of the Land Tax Assessments', *EcHR*, 1st Ser., 1 (1927).
[20] E. C. K. Gonner, *Common Land and Inclosure* (1912).
[21] H. L. Gray, 'Yeoman Farming in Oxfordshire from the Sixteenth Century to the Nineteenth', *Quarterly Journal of Economics*, 24 (1910).
[22] J. L. and B. Hammond, *The Village Labourer* (1911).
[23] A. H. Johnson, *The Disappearance of the Small Landowner* (1909).
[24] V. M. Lavrovsky, 'Tithe Commutation as a Factor in the Gradual Decrease of Landownership by the English Peasantry', *EcHR*, 1st Ser., 4 (1932–4).
[25] ——, 'Parliamentary Enclosures in the County of Suffolk, (1797–1814)', *EcHR*, 1st Ser., 7 (1937).
[26] J. Rae, 'Why have the Yeomanry Perished?', *Contemporary Review*, 44 (1883).
[27] G. Slater, *The English Peasantry and the Enclosure of Common Fields* (1907).
[28] T. H. Swales, 'The Parliamentary Enclosures of Lindsey', *Reports and Papers of the Architectural and Archaeological Societies of*

Lincolnshire and Northamptonshire, in two parts, old series 42 (1937), new series 2 (1938).

(e) BOOKS AND ARTICLES 1940 AND LATER (ENGLAND AND WALES)

[29] R. C. Allen, 'The Efficiency and Distributional Consequences of Eighteenth Century Enclosures', *Economic Journal*, 92 (1982).

[30] W. G. Armstrong, 'The Influence of Demographic Factors on the Position of the Agricultural Labourer in England and Wales, c.1750–1914', *AHR*, 29 (1981).

[31] T. S. Ashton, *An Economic History of England: the Eighteenth Century* (1955).

[32] B. D. Baack, 'The Development of Exclusive Property Rights to Land in England: An Exploratory Essay', *Economy and History*, 22 (1979).

[33] B. D. Baack and R. P. Thomas, 'The Enclosure Movement and the Supply of Labour during the Industrial Revolution', *JEEH*, 3 (1974).

[34] T. W. Beastall, *A North Country Estate: The Lumleys and Saundersons as Landowners 1600–1900* (1975).

[35] J. V. Beckett, 'Regional Variation and the Agricultural Depression', *EcHR*, 35 (1982).

[36] ——, 'The Decline of the Small Landowner in Eighteenth and Nineteenth-Century England: Some Regional Considerations', *AHR*, 30 (1982).

[37] M. W. Beresford, 'The Commissioners of Enclosure', *EcHR*, 1st Ser., 16 (1946).

[38] ——, 'The Decree Rolls of Chancery as a Source for Economic History, 1547–c.1700', *EcHR*, 32 (1979).

[39] B. J. Buchanan, 'The Financing of Parliamentary Waste Land Enclosure: Some Evidence from North Somerset, 1770–1830', *AHR*, 30 (1982).

[40] R. A. Butlin, 'Enclosure and Improvement in Northumberland in the Sixteenth Century', *Archaeologia Aeliana*, 45 (1967).

[41] ——, 'Field Systems of Northumberland and Durham', in A. R. H. Baker and R. A. Butlin (eds), *Studies of Field Systems in the British Isles* (1973).

[42] ——, 'The Enclosure of Open Fields and Extinction of Common Rights in England, c.1600–1750: A Review', in H. S. A. Fox and

R. A. Butlin (eds), *Change in the Countryside: Essays on Rural England, 1500–1900* (1979).

[43] J. D. Chambers, 'Enclosure and the Small Landowner', *EcHR*, 1st Ser., 10 (1940).

[44] ——, 'Enclosure and the Small Landowner in Lindsey', *The Lincolnshire Historian*, 1 (1947).

[45] ——, 'Enclosure and Labour Supply in the Industrial Revolution', *EcHR*, 5 (1953), and reprinted in E. L. Jones (ed.), *Agriculture and Economic Growth in England, 1650–1815* (1967).

[46] J. D. Chambers and G. E. Mingay, *The Agricultural Revolution, 1750–1880* (1966).

[47] J. Chapman, 'Land Purchases at Enclosure: Evidence from West Sussex', *The Local Historian*, 12 (1977).

[48] ——, 'Some Problems in the Interpretation of Enclosure Awards', *AHR*, 26 (1978).

[49] ——, 'The Parliamentary Enclosures of West Sussex', *Southern History*, 2 (1980).

[50] J. Chapman and T. M. Harris, 'The Accuracy of Enclosure Estimates: Some Evidence from Northern England', *Journal of Historical Geography*, 8 (1982).

[51] N. F. R. Crafts, 'Determinants of the Rate of Parliamentary Enclosure', *EEH*, 14 (1977).

[52] ——, 'Enclosure and Labour Supply Revisited', *EEH*, 15 (1978).

[53] ——, 'Income Elasticities of Demand and the Release of Labour by Agriculture During the British Industrial Revolution', *JEEH*, 9 (1980).

[54] C. Dahlman, *The Open Field System and Beyond: A Property Rights Analysis of an Economic Institution* (1980).

[55] H. C. Darby, 'The Age of the Improver: 1600–1800', in H. C. Darby (ed.), *A New Historical Geography of England* (1973).

[56] S. R. Eyre, 'The Upward Limit of Enclosure on the East Moor of North Derbyshire', *TrIBG*, 23 (1957).

[57] R. T. Fieldhouse, 'Agriculture in Wensleydale from 1600 to the Present Day', *Northern History*, 16 (1980).

[58] D. V. Fowkes, 'Mapleton an Eighteenth Century Private Enclosure', *Derbyshire Miscellany*, 6 (1972).

[59] D. B. Grigg, 'Small and Large Farms in England and Wales', *Geography, 48 (1963)*.

[60] ——, 'The Land Tax Returns', *AHR*, 11 (1963).

[61] ——, *The Agricultural Revolution in South Lincolnshire* (1966).

[62] M. Havinden, 'Agricultural Progress in Open Field Oxford-shire', *AHR*, 9 (1961).

[63] R. I. Hodgson, 'The Progress of Enclosure in County Durham, 1550–1870', in H. S. A. Fox and R. A. Butlin (eds), *Change in the Countryside: Essays on Rural England, 1500–1900* (1979).

[64] B. A. Holderness, 'Capital Formation in Agriculture, 1750–1850', in J. P. P. Higgins and S. Pollard (eds), *Aspects of Capital Investment in Great Britain 1750–1850* (1971).

[65] W. G. Hoskins, 'The Reclamation of the Waste in Devon, 1550–1800', *EcHR*, 1st Ser., 13 (1943).

[66] H. G. Hunt, 'The Chronology of Parliamentary Enclosure in Leicestershire', *EcHR*, 10 (1957).

[67] ——, 'Landownership and Enclosure, 1750–1830', *EcHR*, 11 (1958–9).

[68] S. A. Johnson, 'Some Aspects of Enclosure and Changing Agricultural Landscapes in Lindsey from the Sixteenth to the Nineteenth Century', *Reports and Papers of the Lincolnshire Architectural and Archaeological Society*, 9 (1962).

[69] E. Kerridge, *The Agricultural Revolution* (1967).

[70] V. M. Lavrovsky, *Parliamentary Enclosure of the Common Fields in England at the end of the eighteenth century and beginning of the nineteenth* (1940); this is an English translation of the title only. The book has never been translated but see the review by C. Hill, *EcHR*, 1st Ser., 12 (1942).

[71] ——, 'The Expropriation of the English Peasantry in the Eighteenth Century', *EcHR*, 9 (1956–7).

[72] D. N. McCloskey, 'The Enclosure of Open Fields: Preface to a study of its Impact on the Efficiency of English Agriculture in the Eighteenth Century', *Journal of Economic History*, 32 (1972).

[73] ——, 'The Persistence of English Common Fields', in W. N. Parker and E. L. Jones (eds), *European Peasants and their Markets: Essays in Agrarian History* (1975).

[74] ——, 'The Economics of Enclosure: A Market Analysis', in W. N. Parker and E. L. Jones (eds), *European Peasants and their Markets: Essays in Agrarian History* (1975).

[75] ——, 'English Open Fields as Behaviour Towards Risk', *Research in Economic History*, 1 (1976).

[76] J. M. Martin, 'Landownership and the Land Tax Returns', *AHR*, 14 (1966).

[77] ——, 'The Parliamentary Enclosure Movement and Rural Society in Warwickshire', *AHR*, 15 (1967).

[78] ——, 'The Cost of Parliamentary Enclosure in Warwickshire', in E. L. Jones (ed.), *Agriculture and Economic Growth in England 1650–1815* (1967).

[79] ——, 'Members of Parliament and Enclosure: A Reconsideration', *AHR,* 27 (1979).

[80] ——, 'The Small Landowner and Parliamentary Enclosure in Warwickshire', *EcHR*, 32 (1979).

[81] John Martin, 'Enclosure and the Inquisitions of 1607: An Examination of Dr Kerridge's Article, "The Returns of the Inquisitions of Depopulation"', *AHR*, 30 (1982).

[82] D. R. Mills, 'Enclosure in Kesteven', *AHR*, 7 (1959).

[83] G. E. Mingay, 'The Size of Farms in the Eighteenth Century', *EcHR*, 14 (1962).

[84] ——, 'The Land Tax Assessments and the Small Landowner', *EcHR*, 17 (1964).

[85] ——, *Enclosure and the Small Farmer in the Age of the Industrial Revolution* (1968).

[86] ——, (ed.), *Arthur Young and His Times* (1975).

[87] J. L. Purdum, 'Profitability and Timing of Parliamentary Land Enclosures', *EEH*, 15 (1978).

[88] B. K. Roberts, 'Field Systems in the West Midlands', in A. R. H. Baker and R. A. Butlin (eds), *Studies of Field Systems in the British Isles* (1973).

[89] E. and R. Russell, *Landscape Changes in South Humberside: The Enclosures of Thirty-Seven Parishes* (1982).

[90] R. E. Sandell, *Abstracts of Wiltshire Inclosure Awards and Agreements* (Wiltshire Record Society, 25 for 1969 published 1971).

[91] J. Saville, 'Primitive Accumulation and Early Industrialisation in Britain', *The Socialist Register*, 6 (1969).

[92] L. D. Stamp and W. G. Hoskins, *The Common Lands of England and Wales* (1963).

[93] W. E. Tate, 'Members of Parliament and the Proceedings upon Enclosure Bills', *EcHR*, 1st Ser., 12 (1942).

[94] ——, 'Parliamentary Counter-Petitions During the Enclosures of the Eighteenth and Nineteenth Centuries', *English Historical Review*, 59 (1944).

[95] ——, 'Opposition to Parliamentary Enclosure in Eighteenth Century England', *Agricultural History*, 19 (1945).

[96] ——, 'Members of Parliament and Their Personal Relations to Enclosure', *Agricultural History*, 23 (1949).

[97] ——, 'The Cost of Parliamentary Enclosure in England', *EcHR*, 5 (1952).

[98] ——, *The English Village Community and the Enclosure Movement* (1967).

[99] D. Thomas, *Agriculture in Wales During the Napoleonic Wars* (1963).

[100] J. G. Thomas, 'The Distribution of the Commons in part of Arwystli at the Time of Enclosure', *Montgomeryshire Collections*, 54 (1955).

[101] ——, 'Some Enclosure Patterns in Central Wales', *Geography*, 42 (1957).

[102] E. P. Thompson, *The Making of the English Working Class* (1963).

[103] K. Tribe, *Genealogies of Capitalism* (1981).

[104] M. E. Turner, 'The Cost of Parliamentary Enclosure in Buckinghamshire', *AHR*, 21 (1973).

[105] ——, 'Parliamentary Enclosure and Landownership Change in Buckinghamshire', *EcHR*, 28 (1975).

[106] ——, 'Enclosure Commissioners and Buckinghamshire Parliamentary Enclosure', *AHR*, 25 (1977).

[107] ——, *English Parliamentary Enclosure* (1980).

[108] ——, 'Cost, Finance, and Parliamentary Enclosure', *EcHR*, 34 (1981).

[109] ——, 'Agricultural Productivity in England in the Eighteenth Century: Evidence from Crop Yields', *EcHR*, 35 (1982).

[110] ——, (ed.), *Home Office Acreage Returns* (HO67), (List and Index Society in four volumes, 189–90, 1982, and 195–6, 1983).

[111] J. Walton, 'The Residential Mobility of Farmers and its Relationship to the Parliamentary Enclosure Movement in Oxfordshire', in A. D. M. Phillips and B. J. Turton (eds), *Environment, Man and Economic Change* (1975).

[112] M. Williams, 'The Enclosure and Reclamation of Wasteland in England and Wales in the Eighteenth and Nineteenth Centuries', *TrIBG*, 51 (1970).

[113] ——, 'The Enclosure and Reclamation of the Mendip Hills', *AHR*, 19 (1971).

[114] ——, 'The Enclosure of Wasteland in Somerset', *TrIBG*, 57 (1972).

[115] E. M. Yates, 'Enclosure and the Rise of Grassland Farming in

Staffordshire', *North Staffordshire Journal of Field Studies*, 14 (1974).

[116] J. A. Yelling, 'Common Land and Enclosure in East Worcestershire, 1540–1870', *TrIBG*, 45 (1968).

[117] ——, 'Changes in Crop Production in East Worcestershire, 1540–1867', *AHR* 21 (1973).

[118] ——, *Common Field and Enclosure in England 1450–1850* (1977).

(f) SCOTLAND

[119] I. H. Adams, 'The Land Surveyor and His Influence on the Scottish Rural Landscape', *SGM*, 84 (1968).

[120] ——, 'Economic Process and the Scottish Land Surveyor', *Imago Mundi*, 27 (1975).

[121] ——, 'The Agricultural Revolution in Scotland: Contributions to The Debate', *Area*, 10 (1978).

[122] ——, 'The Agents of Agricultural Change', in M. L. Parry and T. R. Slater (eds) ([*140*] *below*).

[123] J. B. Caird, 'The Making of the Scottish Rural Landscape', *SGM*, 80 (1964).

[124] ——, 'The Reshaped Agricultural Landscape', in M. L. Parry and T. R. Slater (eds) ([*140*] *below*).

[125] I. Carter, *Farmlife in Northeast Scotland 1840–1914* (1979).

[126] R. A. Dodgshon, 'The Removal of Runrig in Roxburghshire and Berwickshire 1680–1766', *Scottish Studies*, 16 (1972).

[127] ——, 'Towards an Understanding and Definition of Runrig: the Evidence for Roxburghshire and Berwickshire', *TrIBG*, 64 (1975).

[128] ——, 'The Origins of Traditional Field Systems', in M. L. Parry and T. R. Slater (eds) ([*140*] *below*).

[129] R. A. Gailey, 'Agrarian Improvement and the Development of Enclosure in the South-West Highlands of Scotland', *Scottish Historical Review*, 42 (1963).

[130] I. F. Grant, 'The Social Effects of the Agricultural Reforms and Enclosure Movement in Aberdeenshire', *Economic History*, 1 (1926–9).

[131] M. Gray, 'Scottish Emigration: The Social Impact of Agrarian Change in the Rural Lowlands, 1775–1875', *Perspectives in American History*, 7 (1973).

[132] H. Hamilton, *An Economic History of Scotland in the Eighteenth Century* (1963).

[133] J. E. Handley, *Scottish Farming in the Eighteenth Century* (1953).

[134] ——, *The Agricultural Revolution in Scotland* (1963).

[135] J. H. G. Lebon, 'The Process of Enclosure in the Western Lowlands', *SGM*, 62 (1946).

[136] D. R. Mills, 'A Scottish Agricultural Revolution?', *Area*, 8 (1976).

[137] A. C. O'Dell, 'A View of Scotland in the Middle of the Eighteenth Century', *SGM*, 69 (1953).

[138] M. L. Parry, 'A Scottish Agricultural Revolution?', *Area*, 8 (1976).

[139] ——, 'Changes in the Extent of Improved Farmland', in M. L. Parry and T. R. Slater (eds) (*[140] below*).

[140] M. L. Parry and T. R. Slater (eds), *The Making of the Scottish Countryside* (1980).

[141] T. C. Smout, *A History of the Scottish People 1560–1830* (1969).

[142] ——, Introduction to Sir John Sinclair (ed.), *The Statistical Account of Scotland 1791–99*, Vol. II, *The Lothians* (1975).

[143] T. C. Smout and A. Fenton, 'Scottish Agriculture before the Improvers: An Exploration', *AHR*, 13 (1965).

[144] J. A. Symon, *Scottish Farming Past and Present* (1959).

[145] B. M. W. Third, 'Changing Landscape and Social Structure in Scottish Lowlands as Revealed by Eighteenth Century Estate Plans', *SGM*, 71 (1955).

[146] G. Whittington, 'The Problem of Runrig', *SGM*, 86 (1970).

[147] ——, 'Was there a Scottish Agricultural Revolution?', *Area*, 7 (1975).

[148] ——, 'Field Systems of Scotland', in A. R. H. Baker and R. A. Butlin (eds), *Studies of Field Systems in the British Isles* (1973).

[149] I. D. Whyte, 'The Agricultural Revolution in Scotland: Contributions to the Debate', *Area*, 10 (1978).

[150] ——, *Agriculture and Society in Seventeenth Century Scotland* (1979).

[151] ——, 'The Emergence of the New Estate Structure', in M. L. Parry and T. R. Slater (eds) (*[140] above*).

(g) THESES (see also [3] above, pp. 69–73)

[152] J. R. Ellis, *Parliamentary Enclosure in Wiltshire* (PhD, University of Bristol, 1971).

[153] H. G. Hunt, *The Parliamentary Enclosure Movement in Leicestershire, 1730–1842* (PhD, University of London, 1956).

[154] J. M. Martin, *Warwickshire and the Parliamentary Enclosure Movement* (PhD, University of Birmingham, 1965).

[155] J. M. Neesom, *Common Right and Enclosure in Eighteenth Century Northamptonshire* (PhD, University of Warwick, 1977).

[156] W. S. Rodgers, *The Distribution of Parliamentary Enclosures in the West Riding of Yorkshire, 1729–1850* (MComm, University of Leeds, 1953).

[157] M. E. Turner, *Some Social and Economic Considerations of Parliamentary Enclosure in Buckinghamshire, 1738–1865* (PhD, University of Sheffield, 1973).

[158] J. R. Walton, *Aspects of Agrarian Change in Oxfordshire, 1750–1880* (DPhil, University of Oxford, 1976).

Index

Note: The terms 'parliamentary enclosure', 'open fields' and 'commons and wastes' occur so often as to defy satisfactory indexing.

Aberdeenshire 32, 73, 78
absentee ownership 68, 70, 75
  see also landlords
Acts and Bills
  England and Wales 12, 16–17, 26–7, 29,
    33, 40, 43, 45, 53–4, 59–62, 64
  Scotland 30–2
Adams, I. H. 28
Allen, R. C. 43–4
animal husbandry 27, 38–9, 50–1, 82–3
arable 18, 19–20, 23, 24, 26, 27, 36, 38, 39,
  43, 46, 50–1, 81
Arden Forest, Warwickshire 26
Argyllshire 31
Ashton, T. S. 42, 51
Avon Valley, Warwickshire 26
Ayrshire 28–9

Barton upon Humber, Lincolnshire 40
Berkshire 19
Berwickshire 31, 73
Bishopstone, Buckinghamshire 45–6
Board of Agriculture 23
Bosbury, Herefordshire 41
Bowen, I. 26
Buckinghamshire 38, 41, 45–6, 57–8, 61–3,
  65–6, 70, 75

Caird, J. B. 28
Cambridgeshire 11, 17, 24
capital and capital investment 36, 41–2, 45,
  51–3, 56, 59–60, 69, 82
capitalism, agrarian and industrial 14, 64,
  66, 71, 73, 76, 79
cattle trade in Scotland 30, 73
Chambers, J. D. 33, 47, 67–70, 71–9
church 12, 44, 65–7
  see also tithes
clerks 12, 53–4, 61–3
commissioners 11, 12, 45, 53–5, 58–60, 61–3
common grazing 27
common rights 11, 14, 42–3, 65, 75–6, 80,
  82
Commons Registration Act (1965) 13
commonties 30–2

communal ownership 11, 12, 31, 55, 58,
  79–80
consols, yield on 45, 49–52
cost benefit 41–6
cost of enclosure 12, 45–7, 50, 53–63, 65, 70,
  73–4, 79–80, 82–3
cottagers 65, 68–9, 82–3
Court of Sessions, Scotland 32
Crafts, N. F. R. 78–9
Cumbria 19
Curtler, W. H. R. 14, 63

Darby, H. C. 34
Davies, E. 65, 67–8
Davis, T. 38
demand 36, 77–8, 81
depopulation 34, 39, 77–9
depressions, economic and agricultural 23,
  36, 38–9, 47, 50, 68–9, 76, 78
Derbyshire 38, 67
Devon 24
diffusion of enclosure 50–1
Dobb, Maurice 77
Dorset 16
Downs, the, of Sussex 24
drainage and underdrainage 11, 21, 60
Dunbartonshire 31
Durham 23, 24, 26, 35, 38, 39

East Anglia 17, 19
efficiency gains 41–3, 53, 60, 79–80, 81–2
Elmstone Hardwicke, Gloucestershire 13
enclosure, definition 11
  new employment and labour
    productivity 64, 77–80, 83
  non-parliamentary 12, 16, 33–5
  Tudor enclosures 43
  see also Acts and Bills, cost of, diffusion of,
    financing of, opposition to, supply of
Epping Forest, Essex 23
Ernle, Lord 33
Essex 23

factor prices 46–52, 79–80
fallows 20, 38, 40–1, 43
farmers, see tenants, owner-occupiers

Felden, the, Warwickshire 26
fences and fencing costs 53–6, 59, 60, 61–3, 74, 78, 82–3
fens 11, 23, 24, 81
Fife 32
financing of enclosure 53, 55–6, 58–9, 74, 82
Finchley Common, Middlesex 23
Fitzwilliam estates 41
Forth-Clyde region, Scotland 31
freeholders 12, 66–8, 70, 72

Gloucestershire 13, 24, 40–1
Gonner, E. C. K. 13
grain yields, improvements of 40, 44, 81
Gray, M. 29
Grigg, D. B. 67–8

Hammonds, J. L. and B. 14, 64–5, 75–6, 80
Hartwell, Buckinghamshire 45
Haut Huntre, Lincolnshire 65
Havinden, M. 37
heaths 11, 23, 81
Herefordshire 41
Hessle, East Yorkshire 45
Highlands, of Scotland 29, 31, 78
Hodgson, R. I. 35
Holderness, B. A. 59–60
Homer, Henry 56, 60
Hounslow Heath, Middlesex 23
Hunt, H. G. 47, 69, 70

industry and industrialisation 60, 70, 71, 78, 79–80, 83
inefficiencies of the open fields 37–9, 81–2
infield-outfield 29
inflationary times 24, 43–4, 47, 50, 58, 69
interest rates 42, 45, 47–52, 69

Johnson, A. H. 13
Jones, T. I. J. 26

Kent 58
Kerridge, E. 33–4, 37
Kesteven, Division of Lincolnshire 38, 46, 66
Kincardinshire 31
King, Gregory 72
King's Sedgemoor, Somerset 65

labour supply 60, 64, 69, 73, 76–80, 83
Lake District 19, 23
landless and landlessness 65, 68–9, 70, 80, 83
landlords and landlordism 39–40, 41–4, 46, 51–3, 66–7, 75, 81
land tax assessments 14, 68, 74
land use changes 36, 39, 41, 43, 50–1, 81
Latton, Wiltshire 41
Lavrovsky, V. M. 65–7, 70, 72

leases 43, 75
Lebon, J. H. G. 28
Lee, Sir William 45–6
Leicestershire 17, 34, 39, 47, 57, 67, 69, 70
Levels, the, Somerset 24
Levy, H. 69
Lincolnshire 11, 19, 24, 26, 34, 38, 39, 40, 41, 46, 57–8, 65, 66, 67
Lindsey, Division of Lincolnshire 39, 46, 57–8, 67
Lothians, the 31, 73, 79
Lowlands, of Scotland 29, 31, 36, 73, 78

McCloskey, D. N. 33–4, 37, 42, 45, 50
Mapleton, Derbyshire 38
marginal land 17, 19, 24, 47, 79, 81
marshes 27, 39
Martin, J. M. 36, 56, 59, 68
Marx and Marxism 14, 67, 76–7, 79
Mendip Hills 24
Middlesex 19, 23, 58–9
Midlands, the, of England 11, 17, 24, 29, 34, 39, 41, 47, 65, 67, 74, 77, 81, 82
Military Survey in Scotland 31
Mingay, G. E. 33, 47, 68, 71, 72
money supply 36, 51–2, 81
Monks Risborough, Buckinghamshire 57–8
Montgomery Act of 1770 31
moors 11, 23, 27, 28, 81
mortgages 45, 63, 74

Napoleonic wars 17, 23, 24, 26–7, 29, 32, 36, 43, 47, 50, 51, 58, 60, 66, 67, 68, 69, 73, 74, 76, 78, 81
Norfolk 11, 24
Northamptonshire 17, 26, 34, 40
Northumberland 24, 26
Nottinghamshire 41, 67, 77

O'Dell, A. C. 31
open and close parishes 66–7
opportunity costs 41, 44–5, 51–2
opposition to enclosure 34, 53, 64, 65, 70, 75–6, 79
Otmoor, Oxfordshire 65, 75–6
overstocking and overstinting 37, 38
owner-occupiers 52–3, 67–8, 71, 72–3, 74, 75, 82
Oxfordshire 17, 40, 41, 57–8, 65, 75–6

pasture and pastoralism 19, 20, 23–4, 27, 28, 30, 36, 38, 39, 43, 50–1, 81, 82–3
Peak District 23
peasants and peasantry 14, 66–8, 71–3, 74–6, 82
Pennines and Pennine counties 11, 19, 23, 24, 26
Perthshire 31
population changes 23, 24, 36, 77–8, 81, 83

prices 23, 36, 44, 47–52, 58, 69, 78, 81
productivity 37, 39–44, 60, 74, 79–80, 83
proletariat 14, 64, 70, 71–2, 77
property rights 14, 37, 42–3, 79, 82
Purdum, J. L. 41–2, 44–5

Radipole, Dorset 16
Rae, J. 76
reafforestation 30
redistribution of income 43–4, 66, 82
regulation of the open fields 37–9
Renfrewshire 28–9
rent 39–40, 41–4, 45, 47, 51–3, 69, 79–80, 81
roads 11, 53–4, 59–60, 61–3, 77
Roxburghshire 73
Roy's Map 31
runrig 29–32, 73

sandlands 23
Saville, J. 71–2
Scotland 11, 16, 24, 28–32, 71–3, 78–9
Sedrup, Buckinghamshire 45
Select Committee of 1800 60–1
severalty 11, 32, 38, 40, 56, 82
Sinclair, Sir John 23
Slater, G. 13, 33
small owners 54–6, 66–70, 71–2, 74–6, 80, 82–3
solicitors 54, 60–3
Solway Firth 31
Somerset 11, 23, 24, 36, 47, 55, 59, 65
southern counties of England 19, 23
south-west counties of England 23
squatters 65, 68–9, 80, 83
Standish, Gloucestershire 40–1
Staffordshire 26
stinting 11, 38
Stone, T. 46
Suffolk 24, 66
Surrey 19

surveyors 12, 45, 53–4, 60–3
Sussex 17, 24, 59

Tate, W. E. 14, 19–20, 56, 63, 65
Tees and Tyne valleys 24
tenants and tenant farming 31, 39–40, 43–4, 47, 52, 69, 70, 71–3, 75–6, 78, 81–3
Thomas, J. G. 27
Thompson, E. P. 64
tithes and tithe fencing 12, 39, 44, 45, 53–4, 59–60, 61–3, 65–7, 74
Turner, M. E. 40, 59
turnover of land 74–6, 82–3

Usury, rate of 42, 45

Vale of Aylesbury, Buckinghamshire 39

wages 79–80
Wales 16, 17, 21, 23, 24, 26–7, 29, 71
Walton, J. R. 75
wars, time of 51
    see also Napoleonic wars
Warwickshire 17, 26, 32, 34, 36, 39, 40, 41, 57–8, 61–3, 65, 66, 70, 75
Weald, the, of Sussex 24
Wensleydale, Yorkshire 26, 27
Westbury, Buckinghamshire 57
Whittington, G. 28
Whyte, I. D. 29
Williams, M. 47
Wiltshire 19–20, 41, 57, 59, 61, 67
woodlands 26
Worcestershire 26, 41

Yelling, J. A. 40, 43, 44, 47
yeomanry 76
Yorkshire, East 19, 24, 45
    West 19, 26
Young, Arthur 39–40, 44

96